How To Succeed At

CYCLING

Franz Wöllenmüller

STERLING PUBLISHING CO., INC. NEW YORK

First published in the United States of America in
1982 by Sterling Publishing Co., Inc., Two Park
Avenue, New York, NY 10016

Translated from the German by Beverley
Worthington

© BLV Verlagsgesellschaft mbH, Munich 1980

First published in Great Britain by
Orbis Publishing Limited, London 1982

ISBN: 0-8069-4152-9

Printed in Singapore

Contents

Introduction

It is certainly nothing new for old, apparently forgotten activities to come into fashion again and experience a real boom in an altered form. This has happened recently in many areas. Cross-country skiing, for example, has taken parts of the world by storm. This sport evolved from the original form of skiing.

There have been similar developments in summer sports. Cycling, for example, has been rediscovered. Twenty-five years ago the bicycle was less of a piece of sporting equipment for the normal person than a useful and cheap means of getting around. The so-called 'economic miracle' quickly changed the cyclists into proud car-owners. In the meantime, many car-owners grew weary of driving in heavy traffic queues every weekend. The 'steel horse' became respectable again – with a few extra refinements developed from the racing bicycles of the great cyclists – from Fausto Coppi to Eddy Merckx.

The success of cycle racing has probably contributed to this surprising rebirth of the bicycle, particularly the great stage races and the influence of the well-known 'classic cyclists'. The great cycle races have fascinated people for years and still do. The Tour de France and the Giro d'Italia are important annual events for millions of cycling fans. Interest in the sports cycle has especially profited from this.

Anyone who wants to go in for cycling as a sport should pay particular attention to the theory involved in cycling. This begins as soon as you buy a 'machine', which must have the correct height of frame and seat position.

The useful advice in this book – on all aspects from the equipment and the right technique to training – should help all enthusiastic sports cyclists. The book will also give you many tips on ways to increase your enjoyment of the sport.

This is less demanding than sports cycling, but can be just as fascinating as flying round corners on a racing machine. Because of the construction of the rims and tyres on bicycles, you can ride on even the worst road surfaces. This enables you to cycle away from the 'mad' traffic on the main roads. Cycling is a particularly good way of satisfying man's need for relaxation and it links man's desire for a greater range of activities to the contemplation and rediscovery of nature.

Today's bicycles are technically advanced constructions which, with the help of gears, make cycling child's play.

Here is a tip for those who have grown out of their child's bicycle with stabilizers, but who want to learn how to ride correctly.

Dismantle the pedals and set the saddle so low that your feet easily touch the ground. Now run with your bicycle, pushing forward first with the right foot and then with the left. This way you will learn how to balance and steer very quickly. Then find a lonely path where you can practise in peace with your machine.

The right bicycle for your use

The first and most elementary mistake is usually made when choosing a bicycle. Here the most popular types are briefly classified.

The folding bicycle

A few years ago it seemed as though the folding bicycle would take the world by storm. The folding bicycle is very suitable for short trips around town or for shopping. But even with gears, this relatively heavy type of bicycle with its small, wide tyres, is unsuitable for longer journeys. You need to pedal hard even on the smallest hills. As well as the wheels, which are too small, there is the frame, which was made short to fit into a car boot (trunk). This has resulted in an unfavourable sitting position.

Cycling for pleasure

Above: a well-equipped lady's tourer. Right: a sporty semi-racer with racing handlebars and Dérailleur gears.

The tourer

Although this is called the tourer, it is not suitable for longer journeys. In the past this was one of the only types of bicycle in existence. It is relatively heavy and unbelievably robust with a back-pedal brake; but it has no gears. The standard tourer is very suitable for leisure cycling, but not for long journeys involving steep hills.

The super-tourer

The newest bicycles from the manufacturers are full of promise. They are lighter and run better than the standard tourer. With a good saddle and well-shaped handlebars, there is much more comfort. In addition, they are all fitted with gears.

For some years now there has been a trend towards the so-called lightweight bicycle. This is generally more expensive, but has great advantages. The frame is made of special, extra-light tubing, the pedals are made of light metal and the cranks, handlebars and chain guard are made of aluminium. You can undertake longer journeys much more easily and comfortably with this lightweight bicycle.

The tandem

The tandem is ideal for couples who get on well together. It does take up rather a lot of space, but then two single bicycles also need space. A well-attuned team can reach quite respectable speeds on this machine.

There are also tandems designed as racing models with a 10-speed version of Dérailleur gears. Difference in fitness between partners will not have such an effect with this bicycle. The husband, for example, who always had to wait at the top of every hill for his wife to catch up, can now exert his strength and fitness for her as well.

The semi-racer

Apart from the racing machine, the semi-racer is the sportiest bicycle. It is light but strong. This type has 5, 8 or 10 gears and narrow tyres. The wire tyres are relatively light, but are nevertheless easy to patch, unlike tyres with tubes (see **Repairing a flat tyre** on page 22). Young people are especially keen on the semi-racer, because it comes quite close to their ideal of a racing bicycle and the price is within their reach. Not only do the racing handlebars make it different from the tourer. According to the price, it includes some of the fittings for a racer. Some accessories are no longer made of steel but of durable

Cycling for pleasure

aluminium: rims, handlebars, pedal cranks, pedals, brakes and the hubs. With a luggage carrier, mudguards (fenders) and different handlebars (comfortable touring handlebars instead of the racing ones), this bicycle is very suitable for touring.

Important points on equipment: If at all possible, a person buying or owning a bicycle should pay attention to the following details:

A wide, comfortable, upholstered saddle is not suitable for long journeys since over a period of time it becomes a hindrance. Anyone intending to make long touring trips would be best advised to get a narrow racing saddle. Easy-care plastic saddles, which have a suede cover, have proved very successful.

Anyone who doesn't want to cycle as a sport should choose one of the comfortable touring or training handlebars which are available in varying styles. These are of more use than racing handlebars.

For shorter trips, gym shoes or light shoes are sufficient. Depending on the pedals, for longer cycling trips you will need cycling shoes with hard, reinforced soles so that the teeth of the pedals do not dig into the balls of your feet; these shoes will also transmit power better.

Touring bicycles at a glance

Type of bicycle & suitability	Advantages & disadvantages	Weight	Price
Folding bicycle shopping trips, going around the town	easy to transport, but can only be used for short trips	c 18kg	£75
Touring bicycle short weekend excursions, shopping trips	very strong and stable, but not suitable for long excursions	c 16-17kg	£175
Super touring bicycle mid-distance trips, shopping	strong and comfortable as a lightweight bicycle, also suitable for long tours	c 14-15kg (lightweight bicycle 13kg)	£500
Tandem mid to long-distance trips	available as touring or sports bicycles	c 20-22kg	£400
Semi-racer longer tours, sporting trips	light-running, but still strong bicycle	c 13-14kg	£200

Cycling for pleasure

Position on the bicycle

With normal touring bicycles, unlike racing models, fitting the frame to your dimensions is seldom possible. However, one point is significant for touring cyclists – adjusting the saddle height. (Read about frame height in the section on **Cycling as a sport** on page 62.)

Sitting on the bicycle, support yourself with your hand against a wall or fence to prevent losing your balance. Then press down one pedal to the lowest position. Place your foot (shoe with a flat sole or no shoe) with the heel on the pedal. The correct saddle height is when your foot is almost fully stretched out.

Care of the bicycle

Your bicycle should always be as spick and span as it was on the day you got it. This section is not just about appearance: a bicycle that is looked after well lasts longer, apart from which dirt in the moving parts reduces efficiency and safety.

Cleaning and oiling are necessary
What you need:
- Paraffin (kerosene)
- Paint brush and old toothbrush
- Chrome cleaner
- Sponge and soft cloth
- Special cleaning fluid

The equipment you need to ensure the proper care of your bicycle, which will repay you with longer life.

Cleaning
Apply the special cleaning fluid over all parts of the bicycle. Work it in quickly and then polish it off with a soft cloth. This type of fluid doesn't only dissolve dirt, but also preserves varnish, chrome and metal at the same time.

You should tackle a really dirty bicycle in the following way: with a lot of water, cleaning fluid and a sponge. A sponge is ideal for cleaning the frame, wheels, brakes, handlebars and tyres. Really filthy tyres can be cleaned with a soft brush.

Rinse the bicycle afterwards

Cycling for pleasure

with clean water. If you use a hose for this, don't keep the jet of water on the pedal bearings, since water will penetrate them if you do.

Of course you must rub the bicycle dry after rinsing it. After such a thorough cleaning, you should oil or grease all movable parts and treat the varnish and chrome with a preservative.

Oiling and greasing

The brake cable, the movable parts of the brakes and the gears must be treated regularly with a good bicycle oil. Use bicycle oil because it is made specially for bicycles and does not gum up. On old bicycles you will see a small greasing nipple attached to the pedal bearings. New models are self-lubricating and therefore require no maintenance. They should, however, be checked over by a cycle dealer once a year. In this case, do not use oil since it decomposes the grease.

Cleaning the hub ball bearing

Before you start this work, you should find out from your cycle dealer whether the hubs of your own bicycle have already been greased and are maintenance-free. If so, no cleaning is necessary. With tourers this is not normally the case. Dismantle the wheels to do this and lay them flat. Pour drops of paraffin into the hub on one side, while turning the axis constantly. The paraffin will flow out underneath, thus cleaning the ball bearing. Only when the paraffin flows out clean on the other side is the bearing clean. Do not forget to oil the hub afterwards.

Cycling for pleasure

Tyres

Pumping up the tyres regularly is also part of caring for your bicycle, even when you are not using it. A tyre that is left for a week with a flat becomes cracked and its life is generally reduced. If the air pressure is always the same, the rubber will not split so easily. There are two possibilities: either keep the tyre pressure constant or take the weight off the tyres by using a bicycle stand or by hanging up the bicycle. For both these alternatives you can buy suitable devices from your cycle dealer.

Cleaning the chain

A dirty or rusting chain is not flexible and therefore makes pedalling harder. You will move forwards more slowly while expending the same amount of energy.

You can clean the chain thoroughly with the help of a paint brush or an old toothbrush dipped in paraffin. You will have to soak a really dirty chain in paraffin. To do this, take the chain off and lay it in a shallow metal dish full of paraffin. The length of chain on tourers and sports cycles is normally linked in one place and is easy to separate. Chains on racers must be unriveted with a special tool. After thorough cleaning, grease the chain link by link. Special chain grease is available for this.

Right:
1 *Combination spanner (wrench)*
2 *Tyre levers*
3 *Combination pliers*
4 *Bicycle oil*
5 *Repair kit and rubber solution*
6 *Screwdriver*
7 *Open-ended spanner*
8 *Ring spanner*
9 *Cleaner and rust protector*

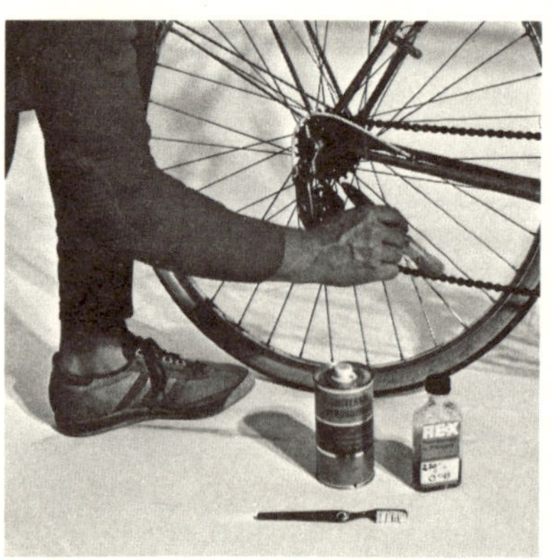

Do not forget to clean the chain properly and regularly. A chain that runs smoothly makes pedalling easier.

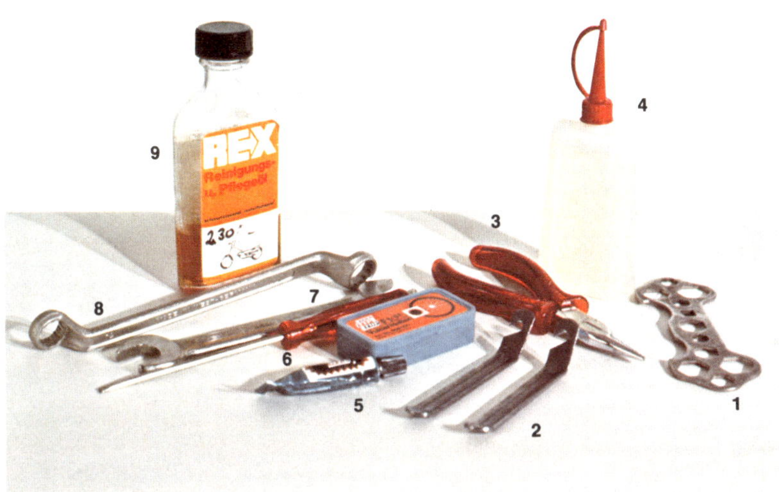

The most important tools

- Combination spanner for 10 different sizes of nut
- Flat 8 or 10-headed spanner
- Screwdriver
- Combination pliers
- Repair kit
- Set of 3 tyre levers

Fitting a brake pad

Properly functioning brakes can save your life. Worn brake rubbers should therefore be replaced regularly. Unscrew the brake pad holder. After removing the old pad, push the

There are many minor repairs you can carry out yourself. The correct tool is a necessary requirement; you can do a lot of damage with bad or unsuitable tools.

Cycling for pleasure

new brake pad into the holder from the side. This is sometimes difficult to do. It will slide more easily with a bit of tallow or a drop of oil. However never get oil on the braking side of the pad, otherwise you will get a nasty shock when you next try to brake.

When fitting a brake-pad holder, you should take care not to fit it the wrong way round – with the open side in the direction the wheel turns. Otherwise the pad will be pushed out again as it rubs on the rim of the wheel.

Adjusting the brakes

If you are taking too long to brake but the pad is still intact, then you must adjust it. With one hand press the brake pads together so that there is a gap of about 3mm

to the rim of the wheel (otherwise the brakes will grip too hard).

Loosen the lower hand nut on the cable control, adjust it and tighten the second nut. If you cannot adjust it any more, loosen the cable clamp screw and pull the brake cable through with a pair of pliers.

Adjusting the handlebars

Release approximately 1cm (or ½in) the screw on the top of the front part of the frame. Give it a light tap with a hammer and you will then be able to adjust the handlebars to the desired height. It is worth testing it out exactly. The following rule can be taken as a reference: two-thirds of your body weight should be borne by the saddle and one third should rest on the handlebars. If the

handlebars are too low, too much weight is loaded on to your arms, which will tire that more quickly and become stiff. If they are too high, you will be in the wrong sitting position; at every slight incline you will have to bend forwards out of the saddle to achieve the best position.

Repairing tyres

Tourers, sports cycles and nearly all semi-racers have so-called 'wired-on' tyres. These tyres consist of two parts: a thinner inner tube which can be pumped up and a strong tyre to protect it. Wired beads are built into the

Cycling for pleasure

edges of these tyres and are measured so accurately that they lie securely on the wheel rim.

The racing cycle has tubular tyres, where the tyre and tube are in one piece. You cannot repair these tubular tyres yourself, so you must take a spare wheel with you on journeys.

For repairing tyres you will need:

- 1 set of tyre levers (3)
- Repair kit and rubber solution
- Rubber patches
- Rasp

Carry out repairs in the following way:

1 First let out any air left in the tyre, then unscrew the valve cap and rim nut; put them safely to one side.

2 Push the smallest tyre lever between the tyre and the wheel rim, followed by the others at 10cm (4in) intervals. Straighten up the levers in turn and notch them into the wheel rim. To take the tyre completely off one side of the wheel rim, push the middle and front levers round bit by bit.

3 When you have taken the tyre off one side of the wheel rim, you can pull out the tube. You will locate the hole more easily if you immerse the tube in a bowl of water or even a deep puddle. Pump up the tube and hold it under the water. Air bubbles will tell you where the damage is in the tube.

Minor repairs

After detaching the wired-on tyre from the wheel rim, you can pull out the tube without much trouble.

You will spot immediately large holes or tears in the tube. But often there are tiny holes from which the air escapes slowly. Pump the tube up gently.

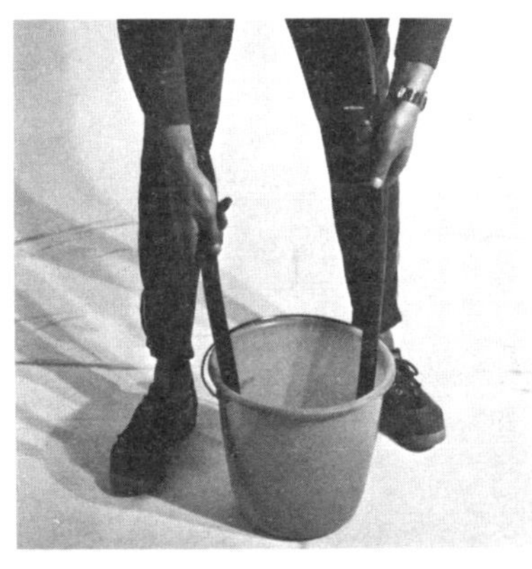

It is best to use a bucket of water to find the damaged area of the tube. Air bubbles rising up in the water indicate the area to be patched.

Cycling for pleasure

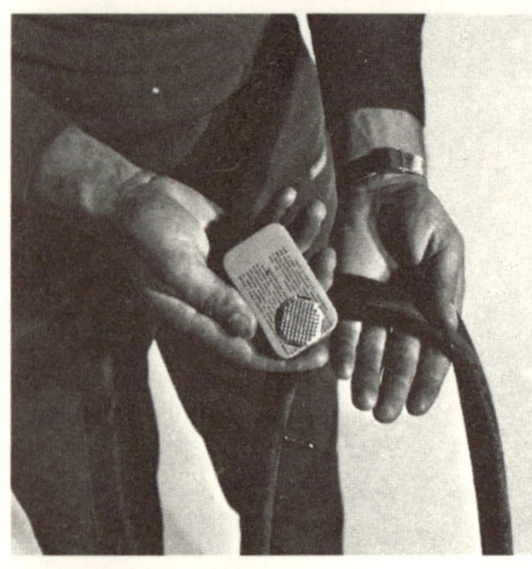

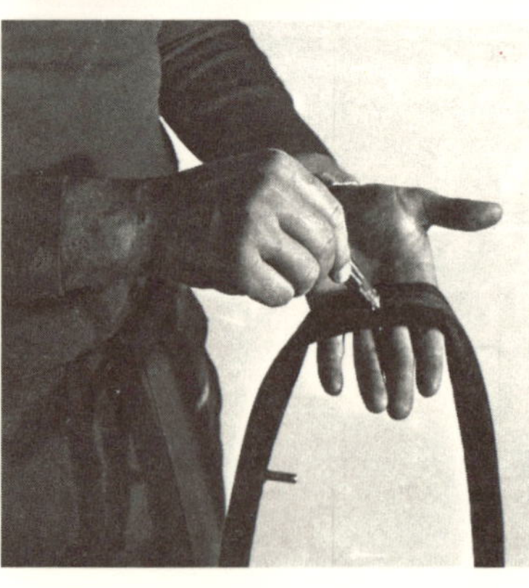

4 If you cannot do the water test, pump up the tube and listen for the sound of escaping air. Alternatively hold the pumped-up tube close to your face and turn the tube round until you feel air escaping. A bit of spit will help you to locate the damaged spot exactly, since it will produce a bubble or two.

5 A small rasp is included in the repair kit and you should use this to roughen the rubber around the damaged area. Spread a thin layer of rubber adhesive the size of the patch on to the tube; this should seal the hole.

6 Leave the adhesive for a few minutes to dry, then remove the protective foil from the rubber patch and press the patch hard on to the damaged area. You should wait about 10 minutes before fitting the tube. When you do this, pump in a little air so that the tube cannot be pinched anywhere. When putting the tyre back on, you should start opposite the valve. With the help of the tyre levers, you should be able to put the tyre back on quite quickly. But take care that the levers do not damage the tube. Before pumping it up again, check that the tyre is not pinching the tube anywhere.

You will soon repair the damage with a good repair kit. You must, of course, take this small kit with you on all cycling trips. Check regularly that the rubber solution is still usable and that you have a sufficient assortment of rubber patches.

1 *Locate the damaged area*
2 *Roughen the rubber*
3 *Spread on rubber adhesive*
4 *Press on the rubber patch*
5 *Insert the tube*
6 *Put back the tyre*
7 *Pump it up with air*

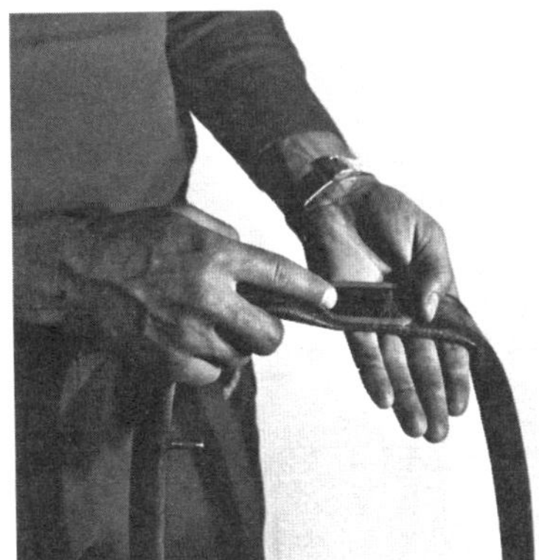

Cycling for pleasure

The lights don't work

One of the chief reasons for accidents at night is no lights or faulty lights on bicycles. A cyclist with no lights cannot be seen by a motorist blinded by an oncoming vehicle.

According to current regulations in Britain, and locally in the United States, bicycles must be equipped for night cycling as follows:

A red reflector to the rear.

A red light to the rear.

A white headlamp above the front wheel spindle, pointing forwards, that can be adjusted.

You should always check, as a matter of principle, that your dynamo (generator) is firmly fitted. Accidents can arise from a loose dynamo getting caught in the spokes of the back wheel.

First test the bulbs. Hold the bulbs between the plus and minus terminals of a flat-shaped battery.

If the lights don't operate in spite of the bulbs being intact, disconnect both cables from the dynamo and check, using the battery.

If the lights work with the battery, the fault lies in the dynamo.

If the lights still don't work with the battery, a defective cable may be the cause. Examine the cables closely for any faulty sections and replace them if necessary.

Anyone who has until now only undertaken short trips will soon want to get to know the surrounding area more closely by bicycle. The tourer or sports bicycle with tough wired-on tyres enables you to plan a journey that also includes good paths and woods. You can spot things from a bicycle that you simply overlook in your car. Many a motorist will agree that until now he or she has sped almost blindly through the countryside and taken in very little of the surroundings. Also, doctors have confirmed the value

Cycling for pleasure

to your health of cycling. Your circulation really gets going when you are pedalling powerfully.

Don't make a lot of fuss over a short cycling trip.

If you take note of a few pieces of advice, you may well derive even more fun from it:

1 Suitable clothes are important in cycling to avoid injuries, as well as coughs and sneezes; not everyone is hardened like a professional racing cyclist. Short trousers or a skirt are only suitable in very warm weather. Otherwise you should wear tracksuit trousers or knee breeches. Wide, flapping trousers get dirty very quickly and can get caught on the chain, resulting in torn trousers or a fall. Shirts and vests must be long enough to cover the back and

kidney area even when bending forwards. You should wear a cap in strong, intense sunlight. You can easily underestimate the effect of the sun because of the wind as you travel along; this can lead to sunstroke.

2 It will only take you a few minutes to give your bicycle a quick check over before your trip. Main trouble spots are the wheel-fixing screws, lights and air pressure in the tyres.

3 No athlete will increase his or her training performance by 100 percent or 200 percent in a day; and if you are not in regular training, you should expect even less of an increase in performance. Don't expect too much at the beginning and bear in mind that a longer way home when you are exhausted can become a torture. Increasing your work load slowly is the correct and healthy way of approaching cycling.

The cycling trip

Going on a long journey is the ambition of many cyclists. Probably you have already done one with friends in your youth. But what is stopping you now from taking a cycling holiday for a few days or even a trip for a few hours? You will have to make certain preparations for a longer trip.

Physical preparation

Although this is the last part of the section on **Cycling for pleasure**, it is nonetheless important, particularly if you are considering a cycling tour. To undertake a tour or even a trip of several days requires some training beforehand.

Touring cyclists who are pedalling away to their destination on their last legs have no time to look at the beauty of the countryside. What should be fun becomes a torture. And it is often difficult for the fit cyclist to be tolerant of a completely unfit member of a touring team.

When taking part in a tour, you must look at yourself realistically and bear in mind your capabilities. On a tour lasting several days, you must consider, above all, your 'seat'. This sensitive part of the body must gradually get accustomed to this type of strain.

How can you increase your fitness? For cyclists going on a tour, regular practice is vitally important. It is better to cover a shorter distance several times a week than longer distances only once or twice. Cycling three or four times a week for an hour is most effective. Anyone who is starting from scratch can work towards the following training and build-up plan:

Cycling for pleasure

Training and build-up plan

1st Week =
2km, 3-4 times in 8-9 minutes

2nd Week =
4km, 3-4 times in 17-18 minutes

3rd Week =
4km, 3-4 times in 16-17 minutes

4th Week =
6km, 3-4 times in 26-28 minutes

5th Week =
6km, 3-4 times in 24-26 minutes

6th Week =
10km, 3-4 times in 45-46 minutes

7th Week =
10km, 3-4 times in 43-44 minutes

8th Week =
12km, 3-4 times in 52-53 minutes

9th Week =
16km, 3 times in 1:10-1:12 hours

10th Week =
20km, 2 times in 1:30-1:31 hours
10km, 1-2 times in 43-44 minutes

Assessment of achievement (in points)

Points	Group 1	Group 2
1 Point	2 km 3:30 min.	2 km 5 min.
2 Points	4 km 7 min.	4 km 10 min.
3 Points	6 km 10:30 min.	6 km 15-16 min.
4 Points	8 km 14-15 min.	8 km 21-22 min.
5 Points	10 km 18:30-19 min.	10 km 27-28 min.
6 Points	12 km 23 min.	12 km 33-34 min.
7 Points	14 km 27 min.	14 km 39-40 min.
8 Points	16 km 31 min.	16 km 45-46 min.
9 Points	18 km 35-36 min.	18 km 51-52 min.
10 Points	20 km 39-40 min.	20 km 57-58 min.

■ Men up to 35 – very fit

■ Men up to 40 – fit

■ Women up to 30 – very fit

11th Week =
20km, 2 times in 1:27-1:29 hours
10km, 1-2 times in 43-44 minutes

12th Week =
30km, 2 times in 1:40-1:42 hours
10km, 2 times in 40-42 minutes

These three months of systematic build-up will put you in a good state of health. You should begin early in the year so that you are fit for cycling's high season.

Using this as a basis, each person can continue as he or she wishes. The following points table should offer some encouragement. Anyone who wants to go on a longer tour of several days should aim to reach the performance achievement of Group 2.

Following pages:
The meeting of different types of transport: the Sardinian peasant with his mule and the cyclist with her modern racing bicycle.

Group 3	Group 4	Points
2 km 7 min.	2 km 8 min.	1 Point
4 km 14 min.	4 km 16-17 min.	2 Points
6 km 21-22 min.	6 km 25-26 min.	3 Points
8 km 29-30 min.	8 km 34-35 min.	4 Points
10 km 37-38 min.	10 km 43-44 min.	5 Points
12 km 45-46 min.	12 km 52-53 min.	6 Points
14 km 53-54 min.	14 km 1:01-1:02 hr	7 Points
16 km 1:01-1:03 hr	16 km 1:10-1:12 hr	8 Points
18 km 1:10-1:12 hr	18 km 1:20-1:21 hr	9 Points
20 km 1:19-1:22 hr	20 km 1:29-1:30 hr	10 Points
■ Men 40-50 – fit	■ Men over 50 – fit	
■ Women up to 40 – fit	■ Women over 40 – fit	
■ Children from 12 – fit		

Cycling for pleasure

The state of your bicycle

If you don't want to experience any unpleasant surprises, check over your bicycle before you set off:

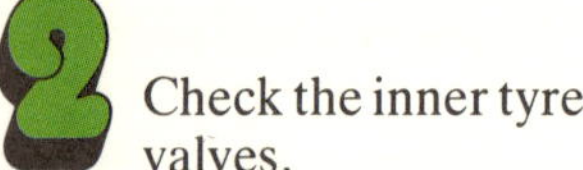

1 Look at the state of the tyres: tyres that are worn or have small fissures (cracks) in the surface should be changed before you set off.

2 Check the inner tyre valves.

3 Check the brakes and adjust if necessary. Perhaps the brake pads need renewing. Don't forget to check the brake cable is tight.

4 Tighten up all screws and check the spokes.

5 Test the lights, since they must be in working order.

6 On long trips, you may need to carry some extra tools and spares with you: two replacement brake pads, a wrench for adjusting the pedal bearing and some replacement spokes. It is also a good idea to take a replacement link for the chain. Replacement light bulbs and a torch (flash light) complete the emergency equipment.

Clothing

When choosing clothes, the considerations of fashion must come last. Clothes must primarily be practical and comfortable. Just think about it: there is never any bad weather unless you are wrongly dressed. You must dress according to the weather. Clothes that are too warm are just as out-of-place as those that are too cool. Absorbent underclothes and a good tracksuit are ideal. For long trips cycling trousers (long or short), such as those that racing cyclists wear, are the most suitable. Sew a soft piece of leather on to the seat to prevent soreness and rubbing. (More details on this are included in the section on **Cycling as a sport**.)

Planning the tour

The cyclist's aims and preferences are crucial when planning a tour. Some prefer to travel keeping closely to a route plan; others let themselves be guided by the roads as they come to them. For most people the happy medium is best. A plan leaving many possibilities open is particularly useful for the inexperienced.

 Keep the first days' stages short while you get acclimatised. Only someone very well trained can recover from a long first stage. For others, the effort of completing the first stage is so great that the following days become a torture.

A 1:100,000 – or, better still, 1:50,000 – map is particularly useful for planning a tour, together with a map distance gauge (see photograph below). With this map aid, you do not need to make elaborate and awkward distance measurements. As a cyclist, you must also be able to map-read: 30km (19 miles) of flat road are child's play; 30 kilometres with steep hills can turn out to be a day's stage. A good map also helps to identify traffic-free side roads. Unsurfaced, good trails are accessible to a cyclist with a touring bicycle. However, things that are not drawn in on the map will constantly surprise even the experienced map-reader. This makes a tour of this kind so fascinating.

Weather conditions and sightseeing slow down the route plan, so you must allow for these. Always be prepared for an extra night's stay.

Cycling for pleasure

How to pack knapsacks and bags

If you pack in whatever seems necessary, you will find that even the largest knapsack will be too small. You must be ruthless about sorting out items if this happens.

All the really necessary items should be packed as follows:

Small bag – fastened on to the handlebars – will take any items you want within easy reach: map of trails, cap, sunglasses, repair kit, camera, sun cream and some provisions.

Twin saddlebags should be fitted on the rear wheel – on the left and right of the luggage carrier. You should pack the following equipment: clothing, raincoat, tool kit, food, spare parts and camping equipment as necessary. (There are extra-light, quick-to-erect tents for mountain climbers that are also very useful for touring cyclists.) When packing twin saddlebags you must distribute the weight evenly. You should observe one basic principle: less luggage means less expenditure of energy, greater comfort on your bicycle and faster speeds.

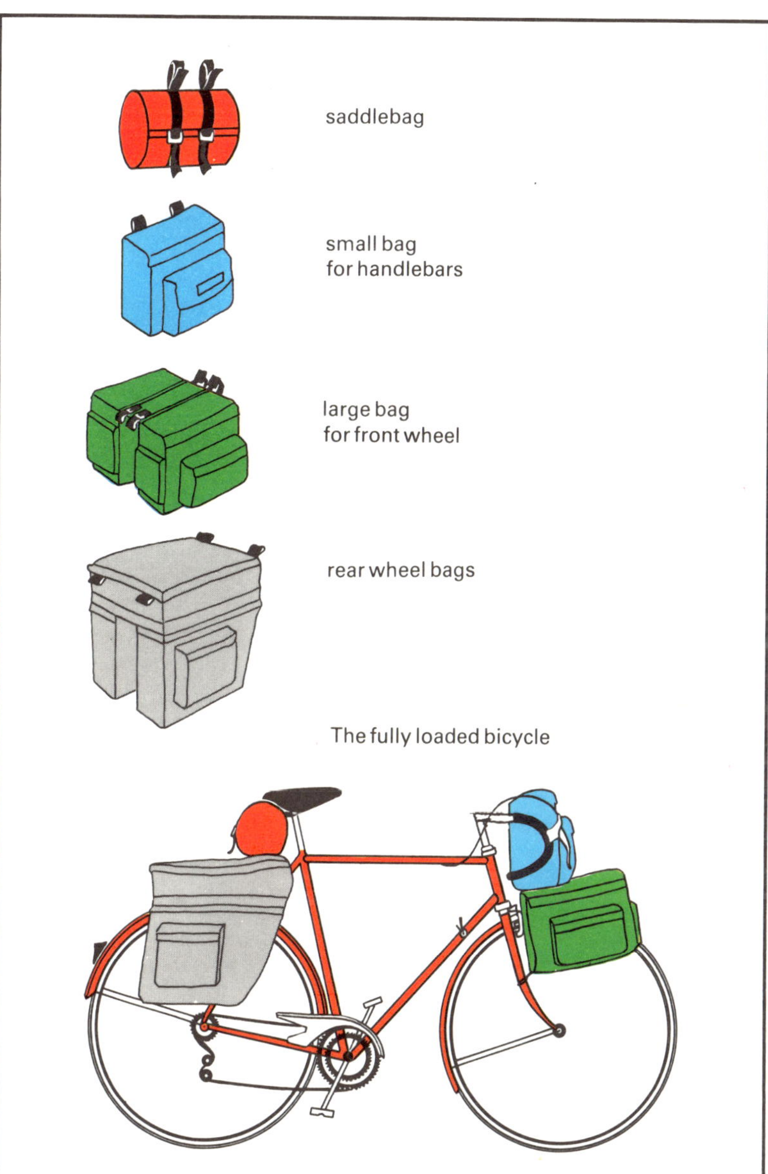
saddlebag
small bag
for handlebars
large bag
for front wheel
rear wheel bags
The fully loaded bicycle

Cycling for pleasure

Cyclists are not alone on the roads

It would be too much to detail all the traffic regulations here. This book cannot replace a close study of the traffic regulations. As a driver you should know all the 'dos' and 'don'ts'. As a cyclist you are the most vulnerable road-user, apart from pedestrians. What results in damaged metal in a collision between two cars can have far more serious consequences if a bicycle is involved. It is in your own interests to bear in mind other road-users. A cyclist rides better when he or she is aware of the situation and keeps both eyes open, especially when travelling through a town or at other critical spots.

(You can learn more on road conduct in the section on **Cycling as a sport.**)

In exceptional circumstances, such as the great international cycle races, other traffic pulls aside to let the cyclists pass. Normally, however, it should always be remembered that cyclists are the most vulnerable road users of all.

Cycling and your health

What doctors say about cycling

Cycling is a very economical means of transport. The weight of the body is borne by the saddle, therefore the work of the legs, which are otherwise needed to hold the body upright, can be converted into energy. It is particularly suitable as a sport for the overweight: the weight of the body is not on the legs but on the saddle. Therefore there is no loss of motion.

The energy consumption of a racing cyclist at speeds of over 40km/hr (25mph) is extremely high since large groups of muscles are working rhythmically and dynamically against resistance.

But even at the lower speeds achieved by spare-time cyclists, the heart, circulation, breathing and metabolism are exercised. Cycling increases strength in the leg and pelvic muscles too. The high intake of oxygen confirmed by tests on racing cyclists is a point in favour of this type of sport as exercise. The heart becomes a powerful and efficient muscle.

One great advantage of cycling is the way overloading can be measured. As in any training, particularly in endurance sports, value should be placed on the correct build-up of training by slowly increasing it. Otherwise there is a danger of over-training.

Other sports, such as swimming, gymnastics and running, should be kept up to enable you to loosen up and give thorough general exercise to the body. Cycling has great value as a sport for the family and as prevention against illnesses due to lack of exercise until well on in life.

With appropriate clothing and proper road sense, cycling is a sport for any age. As in other sports, you should guard against being too ambitious. Covering a distance that is too long and too difficult becomes a torture. You can even damage your health this way.

Cycling as a sport

The racing cycle is growing more and more in popularity as a type of bicycle. The trend is definitely towards cycling as a sport. What is already a tradition in countries such as Belgium, France, Holland and Italy, where cycling is a big sport, is now catching on here.

There the 'giants of the road' are idols for young and old. There are various reasons for the undreamt-of upsurge in popularity. Endurance sports are enjoying increasing popularity, whether it is a question of running, skiing or cycling. And one sport undoubtedly profits from another.

The achievements of our amateur and professional cyclists during recent years also play a large part in this. Famous professional sportsmen and sportswomen will always inspire others to take up that particular sport.

The classic races – Tour de France, Giro d'Italia, Mailand-San Remo, Paris-Roubaix, Fleche Wallonne and the Milk Race, to name but a few – prove the merciless toughness of professional cycle racing. The almost unimaginable personal achievements by cycling professionals have also served to win a special place in the history of the sport. The riders whose achievements go back decades are particularly remembered:

Alfredo Binda, Gino Bertali, Fausto Coppi from Italy; the Frenchman Louison Bobet; the Belgians Rik van Looy and Rik van Steenbergen; the Luxemburger Charly Gaul; the Swiss Hugo Koblet and Ferdi Kubler.

In recent times a new group of cyclists have emerged and hit the headlines: the Frenchmen Jacques Anquetil, Raymond Poulidor, Bernard Thevenet and Bernard Hinault; the Spaniard Frederico Bahamontes; the Belgians Eddy Merckx, Roger Devlaemink, Freddy Maertens, Lucien van Impe; the Italians Felice Gimondi, Francesco Moser; the German riders of the post-war era Rudi Altig, Hennes Junkermann, Rolf Wolfshohl, Diertrich Thurau, Klaus-Peter Thaler, Gregor Braun; and the British riders Reg Harris, Tom Simpson, Norman Shiel.

But the history of this sport would fill a book.

Eddy Merckx, the most successful racing cyclist of all time. The list of his successes is unsurpassed. This great man was the most successful cyclist for seven years (1968-1975). Here are only a few of his successes: 3 times professional world champion, 5 times winner of the Tour de France and 5 times winner of the Giro d'Italia.

Racing saddle
Narrow, light
tubular tyres
10-gear
mechanism

The racing bicycle

Cycling as a sport

Today's racing bicycles represent major technical achievements, which are expensive. The price varies between £500 and £1000. The top price is for bicycle snobs who care more about admiring their machine than sporting achievement.

Taking price increases into account, you will probably have to lay out between £660 and £750 for a good model. Bicycles in this price range are ideal for satisfying sporting ambitions. Cycling fans should not forget that very light constructions are naturally sensitive. If you lay out so much money, you will want to have long-lasting, unspoilt enjoyment of your machine and should therefore treat it with care.

Parts of the racing bicycle

- Frame
- Fork
- Pedal bearing, sprocket wheels, cranks
- Pedals, toe clips, straps
- Control unit – handlebars with head set
- Gears
- Chain
- Rim of the gear
- Brakes and brake levers
- Wheels – wheel rims, hubs, spokes, tyres
- Saddle support
- Saddle
- Bicycle pump, bottle holder

Frame and forks

The frame consists of individual tubular parts connected to one another by so-called 'muffs' or sleeves. These one-piece steel tubes are of different strengths and taper (not visibly) in general conically (for example 0.6/0.9 or 0.6/0.8). These essential parts of racing bicycles are built with various angle dimensions, depending on the country of manufacture.

A frame consists of:
- Horizontal/upper tube or crossbar
- Saddle or seat tube
- Slanting or down tube
- Steering or head tube
- Pedal bearing housing
- Rear set
- Fork
- Drop-outs (they take the front and rear wheels)

Pedal bearing, sprocket wheels, cranks

The pedal bearing on racing machines is made of light metal. Modern materials (titanium, for example) are extremely light, but correspondingly expensive. The two sprocket wheels normally have between 40 and 54 teeth (see **Transmission** on page 74). The right crank has 5 arms bolted to

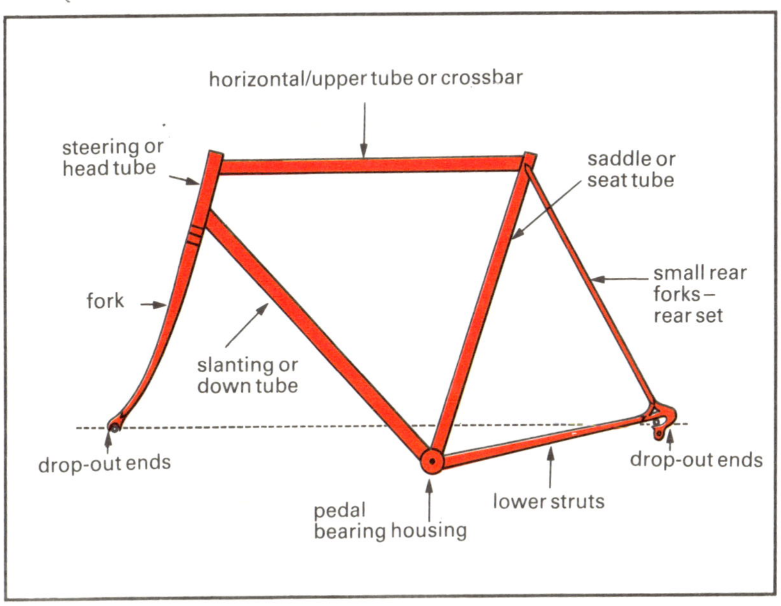

the sprocket wheels. There are cranks of different lengths (see **A bicycle to measure** on page 65).

Pedals, toe clips, straps

The non-expert recognizes a road-racing bicycle primarily from its toe clips and lack of mudguards. The pedals – made of aluminium – must be wide enough to take a full-width shoe (important for cyclists with very large feet). Toe clips come in various sizes – according to shoe size (see **A bicycle to measure**). A safety lock on the end of the racing straps allows you to pull

them tight and release them easily. Many cyclists wrap the end of the strap round with handlebar tape. You can then grasp the tight strap more easily. Wrapping the strap round underneath the lock stiffens it, thereby keeping the small cage open.

Cycling as a sport

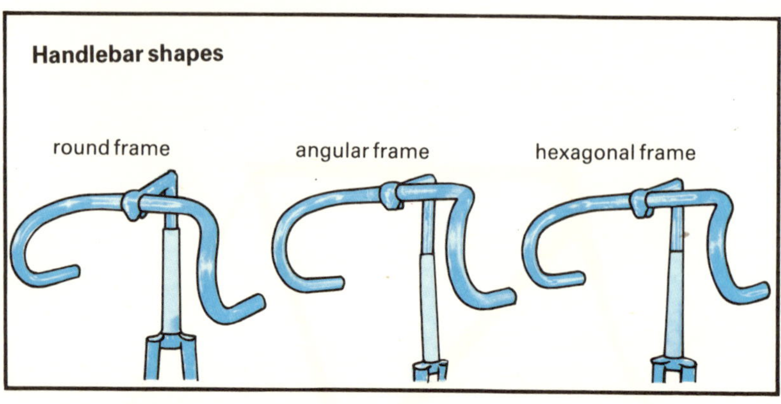

Steering unit

At the top end of the steering or head tube is the steering unit, which holds the head set and handlebars.

Handlebars and head set

The handlebars and head set – also made in light metal – can be bought in various dimensions to suit the main construction of the bicycle (see **A bicycle to measure**). Experts differentiate between racing frames.

The round frame

This was developed before the last war by the Frenchman Pelissier and used by Anquetil, Poulidor and Pigneon among others. This type is particularly suitable for endurance and cross-country cyclists. Long journeys with your hands on the frame are somewhat uncomfortable because of the steep curve. If you have your hands low down, you will have an aerodynamically advantageous position, however.

The angular frame

Eddy Merckx and Felice Gimondi have used this type of handlebar. It creates a good position for the hands above and an aerodynamical body position low on the handlebars. The top cyclists and sprinters like using this frame.

The hexagonal frame

The Italians changed this frame, which was first used by the French and Belgians, and made it rounder. This model allows a very relaxed position with the grip over the brakes. To give the

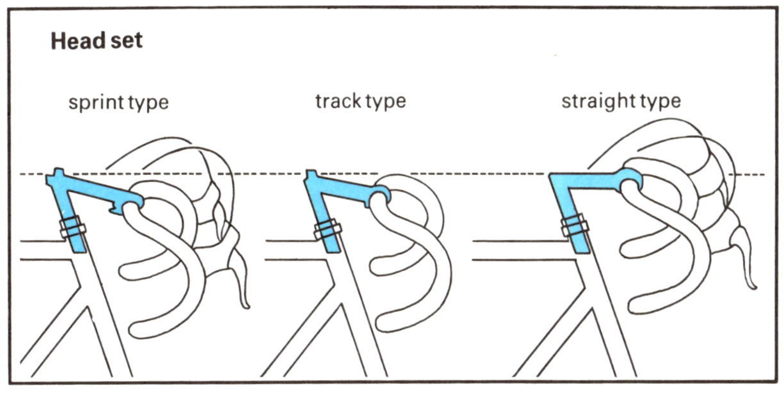

cyclist a better grip on the handlebars, the frame has handlebar tape wrapped round. To avoid injuries in a fall, the frame ends are finished off with rubber stoppers.

The head set of a racing bicycle.

The head set

The so-called head set, together with the 'internal clamp', produces a join between the handlebars and the frame. The head set tube consists of aluminium and, horizontally, is between 6 and 14cm (or 2 and 5in) long (see **A bicycle to measure** on page 68). Not only the length, but also the angle of inclination can be different.

The sprint type, which slopes very sharply downwards, is reserved for sprinters.

The track-racing type only slopes gently downwards.

The straight type is used by all other cyclists and is ideal for spare-time cyclists.

Cycling as a sport

Gears, rim of the gear, chain

The gears consist of the gear levers, gear cables, sprocket wheel gears and the gears for the rear rim of the gear. A racing machine generally has 10 gears (2 sprocket wheels and 5 gear rims) and exceptionally 12 gears (2 sprocket wheels and 6 gear rims) or 18 gears (3 sprocket wheels and 6 gear rims). For the normal cyclist 10 gears is quite sufficient. This offers many types of transmission for all conditions. (For further information, see page 72.)

Chains on road cycles ($\frac{1}{2}$in $\times$ 3/22in) are riveted. The length of chain is tested by laying the chain on the largest gear rim at the front and at the back (this position is not good for cycling – see page 106). In this position the chain has to lie taut, but not too tight.

With longer use and frequent journeys in hilly areas, the chain stretches. You can easily check this: if the chain can be pulled more than 2mm forwards at the edge, then it is ready to be renewed. It is worth replacing the chain regularly: it is subjected to greater wear than the gear rim.

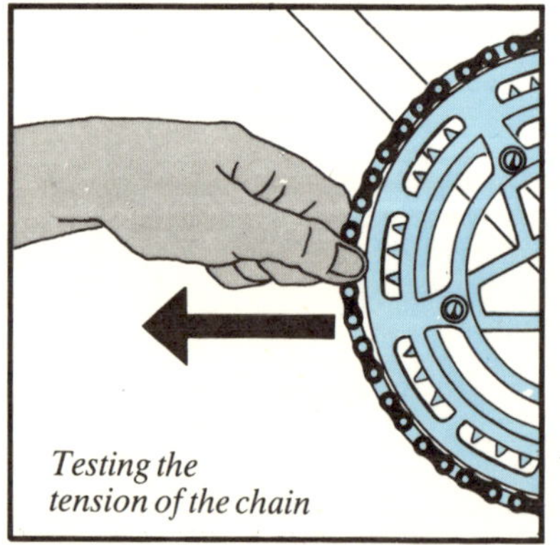

Testing the tension of the chain

The racing bicycle

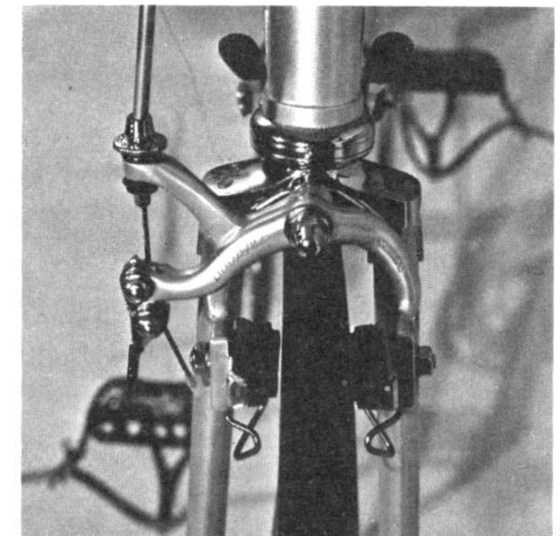

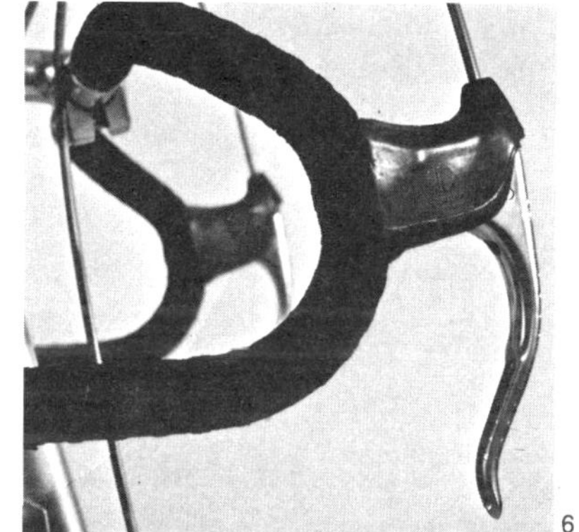

The racing machine consists of many precision units:

1. *Extra-light wheels and tyres*
2. *Pedal bearing and sprocket wheels made of light metal*

3/4 10 or 12 gears

5. *Wheel-rim brakes*
6. *Racing handlebars with partially covered brake grips*
7. *Saddle support and special racing saddle*

Cycling as a sport

Brakes and brake grips

There are two different types of brakes used in racing:

- Centre-gripping wheel rim brakes
- Side-gripping wheel rim brakes

The trend is towards side-gripping brakes. You should pay particular attention to properly functioning brakes and sound brake pads. Defective brakes can lead to serious accidents. New models have a rapid release system. This mechanism enables you to open the brake pads to exchange the wheel.

Wheels – wheel rims, spokes, hubs, tyres

By wheels, we are referring to everything connected with them – wheel rims, spokes, hubs and tyres.

Wheel rims/spokes

As a spare-time cyclist you should strike a balance between the light weight of the wheel rim and its stability. A good average weight is between 300g and 400g per wheel rim. The usual wheel rim has 36 holes – and therefore 36 spokes. You can also get wheel rims with 32, 28 or 24 spokes. Naturally these do not have the stability of a 36-spoke wheel. The

reason for the low number of spokes is not only the decrease in weight because of the reduction in the number of spokes; there is also a substantial decrease in air resistance. Body weight also has a large part to play. Heavy cyclists need a stable wheel.

These points should be weighed up before buying. Bad road surfaces or an indifferent cycling technique quickly lead to a buckled wheel if there are less than 36 spokes. You will then have to centre the wheel by tightening or loosening the spoke nipples.

Despite the advantages of having a cycle with less weight, the basic principle should still apply:

The right wheel rim for the right purpose and cyclist.

Thirty-two spokes should be the minimum number for spare-time cyclists.

Hubs

There is a difference between hubs with a high and low flange. The flange is the edge of the hub that takes the spokes. Spokes of different lengths are used

Cycling as a sport

according to the type of hub. For wheel rims that have less than 32 holes, hubs with a high flange are necessary since they give the bicycle more strength. You should make sure, if fitting spokes, that one spoke crosses over the next three. On racing bicycles, one spoke crosses over the next four. To prevent spokes getting stuck anywhere in the event of a breakage, professionals fit cross-over points with specially designed small metal clips or string. There is, of course, always an exception to every rule. For example, the former Danish world speed record holder Ole Ritter preferred not to fit his spokes with cross-overs when he competed in Mexico in 1974.

The hubs have, in addition, a so-called 'rapid tensioning device'. The wheels are fixed on or released from the ends of the drop-out by just pressing them on or folding back a lever.

Tyres

In road racing, tubular tyres are used; the tube and tyre are made in one piece. Weight plays a large part in the moving parts of a bicycle and the trend is for lighter, and so quicker, machines. However, tubular tyres have the same problems as the wheel rim: low weight and stability work against one another. Therefore compromises have to be made.

Some tubes are made of cotton and silk. The latter is really only used in track racing and on particularly good roads. As a happy medium, a tyre used in cycling as a sport should not weigh less than 300g – and never below 250g. Bear in mind also that the extra-light tyres are correspondingly higher in price.

Here is a tip on how to increase the life of a tyre. Tubular tyres that have been stored dry for a longish time can take substantially more wear and tear than brand new ones (tyres that have just come off the production line to be sold by the dealer). Their performance per kilometre is better and foreign bodies cannot penetrate so easily.

You should have at least one set of tyres in reserve, stored in a cool, dark, dry room. Therefore a cellar with a boiler in would not be suitable. Professionals store tyres mounted on old wheel rims. You can get discarded wheel rims with no spokes from your cycle dealer. You should pump up the tyres from time to time so that they keep their shape.

Saddle support, saddle

The saddle support fits into the saddle tube and is fixed in place after the correct height adjustment has been made. The conventional saddle supports with a toothed system rarely enable the saddle to be correctly adjusted horizontally. With one tooth, the point of the saddle is pointing upwards; with the next tooth it is pointing downwards. With modern saddle supports you can make precise adjustments (see **A bicycle to measure**). Thrifty cyclists must dig rather deeper into their pocket for a racing saddle.

Since the all-leather saddle is relatively hard and needs looking after, especially after rain, saddles of man-made materials are being used more and more. The basic plastic shape is upholstered most easily with foam material and a cover made of smooth leather, suede or buffalo skin is stretched over it. **Some advice:** smooth leather is worth the money, but is slippery; suede is very comfortable, but wears more quicly than buffalo skin. With saddles, you can as a rule assume that the more expensive models are also of better quality.

Bicycle pump, bottle holder and spare tyre

The bicycle pump, bottle holder and drinking flask complete the basic equipment.

A sports cyclist also carries a spare tyre under the saddle or in the bottle holder; this is kept folded up in a cloth bag or a leather case. To ensure this spare tyre is kept in good condition, you should take it out of its bag regularly and pump it up.

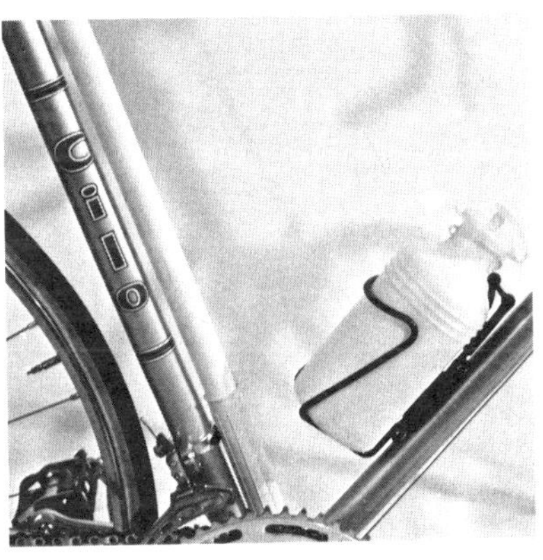

Bicycle pump and bottle are usually fixed to the saddle or lower tube.

Cycling as a sport

A racing frame is soldered to precise measurements. The highest degree of accuracy is necessary for the best quality work.

The final assembly of the frame, which requires skilled craftsmanship. Good frame-builders are highly sought-after.

As in modern car construction, the frames are sprayed automatically and with electrostatic charging.

How a racing bicycle is made

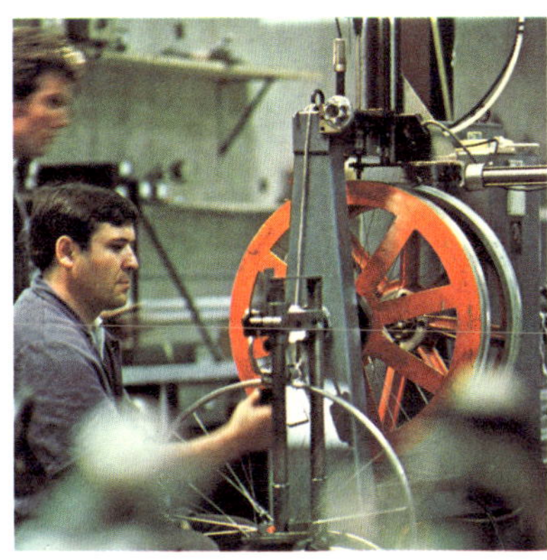

Fitting in spokes and aligning the wheels also require expert skill. A lot of experience and the greatest precision are necessary to ensure the wheels run cleanly and smoothly.

Assembling the many individual parts is the next step in producing a racing bicycle. Some parts are not produced by the cycle manufacturer, but are fitted on by experts according to the customer's requirements.

Close checks on quality and proper working are carried out at the factory after assembly. These should guarantee that no assembly faults can, within reason, threaten the cyclist's safety.

A bicycle to measure

You can spend a lot of money and still not get the best equipment. A cyclist can invest an enormous amount in a road-racing bicycle without being sure that it is right for his or her size. It is essential that a racing bicycle fits exactly.

Of course not everyone needs a made-to-measure frame. For people with a normal build there is an extensive range of ready-made frames to suit. In most cases the spare-time cyclists can also be catered for with these. (There are cycle manufacturers who claim in their advertisements that the stars use quite normal, standard bicycles.)

What parts of the bicycle are important in terms of getting the right size?
- Frame dimensions
- Length of pedal cranks; height of head set to the saddle; saddle further forwards or to the rear
- Racing straps – wide or narrow
- Position of the feet on the pedals
- Transmission

Gregor Braun and Dietrich Thurau appear almost as one with their racing bicycles. A prerequisite for good performances is adapting your bicycle as precisely as possible to your body size.

The right frame

For equipment in other sports (for example, skiing) there are generally details that, apart from minor variations, are valid for all manufacturers and dealers. This does not apply to the construction of racing frames. The dimensions of models from a few manufacturers are prized as closely guarded secrets. If they showed their hand, it would be all to the good of cycle racing.

The important dimensions of racing frames are:
- Frame height
- Length of the crossbar

In standard bicycles – as already mentioned – the height of the frame and the crossbar are in proportion. If you buy a frame that is too high, it is almost certainly too long as well.

Only professional cyclists with unusual body measurements have special frames. Only if you need one (for sprinting or racing in mountainous areas, for example) and can get it cheaply should you buy a specialist's frame.

The right frame measurements ensure a good seat and the correct feeling of balance. The sizes of individual parts of the body are crucial: length of the legs, the arm length and the length of the upper part of the body. The Swiss bicycle manufacturers Cilo have

Cycling as a sport

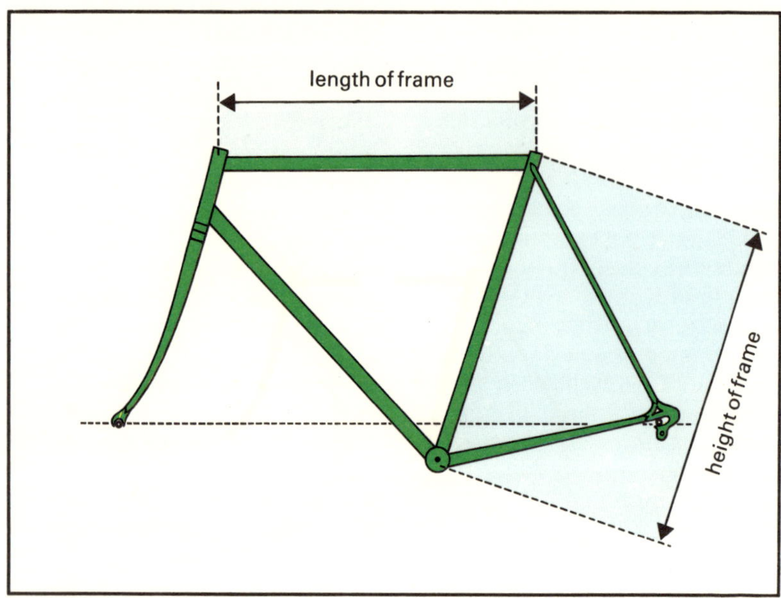

produced a chart from which you can extract individual frame measurements to suit you.

Right: these two diagrams show, in slightly exaggerated form, the right and wrong sitting positions. They correspond to actual sitting positions and were drawn from X-ray pictures. The normal position shows a relaxed spine. The wrong frame, which is too short, can lead to damage to the spine over a long period, as the diagram clearly shows.

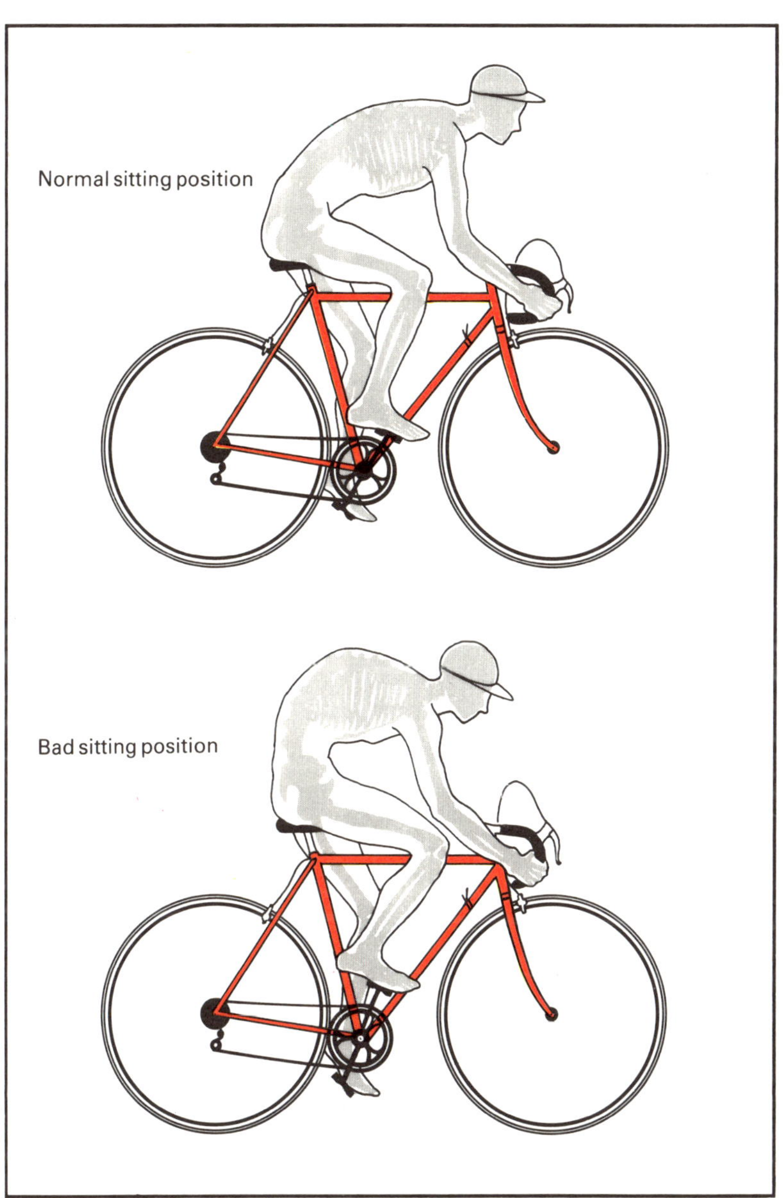
Normal sitting position
Bad sitting position

Cycling as a sport

Frame height

The length of your legs is measured (without shoes) from the ground to the end of your thigh bone, which can easily be felt. You can work out the correct frame height from the chart according to this measurement (A). Frames are all made rather lower today than some years ago. Experience has proved that your feeling of balance and transmission of power are better with lower frames.

Frame length

The sum of the measurements of the upper thigh bone and shoulder height plus the wrist and shoulder height (B+C) gives the necessary information to determine the frame length.

Note: normally the frame height is measured from the centre of the pedal bearing up to the upper edge of the seat tube. But there are manufacturers who measure from the centre of the pedal bearing up to the centre of the crossbar. You should look carefully at the details in leaflets about the machine or check with your dealer for information.

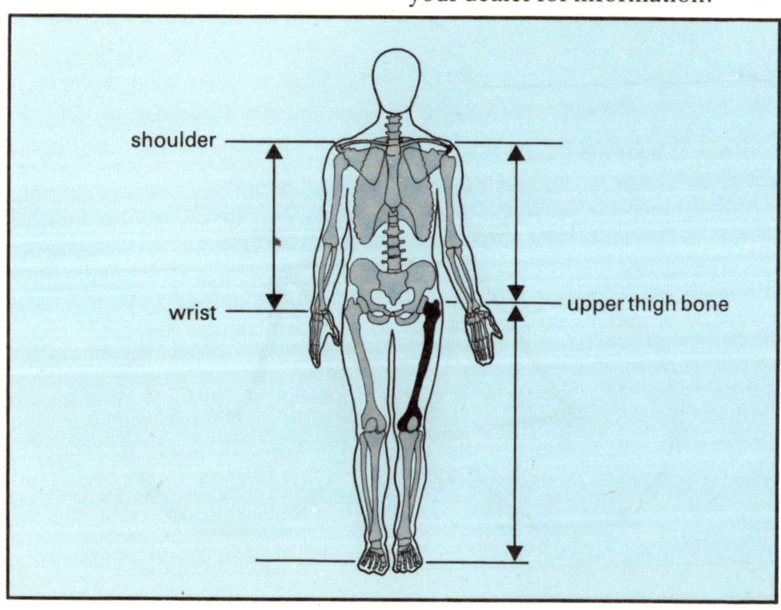

A bicycle to measure

A

length of leg cm	frame height cm
80	51
81	51.7
82	52.4
83	53.1
84	53.7
85	54.3
86	54.9
87	55.5
88	56.1
89	56.7
90	57.5
91	57.9
92	58.5
93	59
94	59.5
95	60
96	60.5
97	60.9
98	61.3
99	61.7
100	62.1

B + C

length of torso and arms cm	frame length cm
100	53
101	53.4
102	53.8
103	54.1
104	54.4
105	54.7
106	55
107	55.3
108	55.6
109	55.9
110	56.2
111	56.5
112	56.8
113	57.1
114	57.4
115	57.5
116	58
117	58.3
118	58.6
119	58.8
120	59
121	59.2
122	59.4
123	59.6
124	59.8
125	60

Length of pedal crank

The cyclist sets the bicycle in motion using muscle power – via the pedal cranks. The length of the pedal crank is therefore crucial to ensure the correct leverage. Fortunately the differences here are not too great.

Normally pedal cranks are 170mm (7in), measured from the centre of the pedal bearing to the centre of the pedal axis. Cyclists with extremely long or extremely short legs are exceptional. Measurements vary from 165mm to 175mm; therefore 1cm (or ½in) separates the shortest from the longest crank.

Ford
Ford
FORD
FRANCE
HUTCHINSON

A bicycle to measure

You should ignore the old rule that the crank should be approximately one tenth of the weight of your body. Tall cyclists would have dangerously long cranks according to this maxim.

The cyclist's strength is relevant here. A very muscular cyclist can use long cranks better than one with less strength.

The following tips could be useful for you:

 Small cyclists who use a frame of 50-55cm should choose a crank 165mm long.

 Medium-sized cyclists who use a frame of 56-59cm need pedal cranks 170mm long.

 Tall cyclists using frames of 60-61cm should choose 170mm-175mm long cranks.

Saddle position

It is very easy to adjust the height of the saddle. Sit straight on the saddle, supporting yourself with one hand against a wall or fence. Now place your heel (with cycling shoes) onto the pedal. In the lowest position your leg should be virtually fully extended. If so, the height of the saddle is correctly adjusted. When pedalling, the ball of the foot is on the pedal, thus reducing the distance. To prevent the height of the saddle altering because of screws not being tight enough, simply stick a strip of handlebar tape on the lowest part of the saddle support.

A saddle that is too low can cause pain in the thigh muscles above the knee. One that is too high can lead to trouble in the fibula and pain between the legs.

According to the experts, the saddle is correctly adjusted when you can cycle downhill very quickly without bouncing out of the saddle and cycle uphill without feeling that you have to stand up.

The Frenchman Jacques Anquetil belongs to the greats of cycling with his five victories in the Tour de France. Two victories in the Giro d'Italia number among his other successes.

Cycling as a sport

Should the saddle be further forwards or backwards?

The position of the saddle in relation to the handlebars and the pedal bearing is essential for a comfortable and correctly positioned seat. The saddle can be positioned towards the front or the back. The following points can be used as a rule of thumb: the measurements of the upper edge of the saddle/axis of the pedal bearing and the point of the saddle/lower curve of the handlebars are roughly the same.

A further point: when the pedals are horizontal, hold a plumb-line at the point of the knee. The plumb line should meet the centre of the axis of the pedal. The often quoted way of measuring – with your hand outstretched and your elbow laid on to the front of the saddle, the fingertips must be 2cm (or 1in) from the frame – is too imprecise.

Adjusting the height of the saddle accurately is very important.

Height of head set and saddle

There is also a correct line for this measurement: the upper edge of the saddle should be at its highest 3cm (or 1½in) above the head set. At the beginning of training early in the year some cyclists set the saddle and head set at the same height. Then, as their form improves during training and their muscles become toned up, they lower the head set.

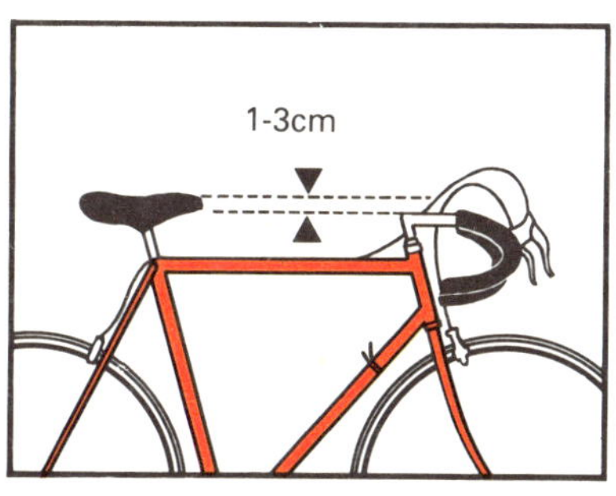

Below: the distance from the point of the saddle to the head set is part of other criteria. The text and diagram (above) show when the distance is correct.

Cycling as a sport

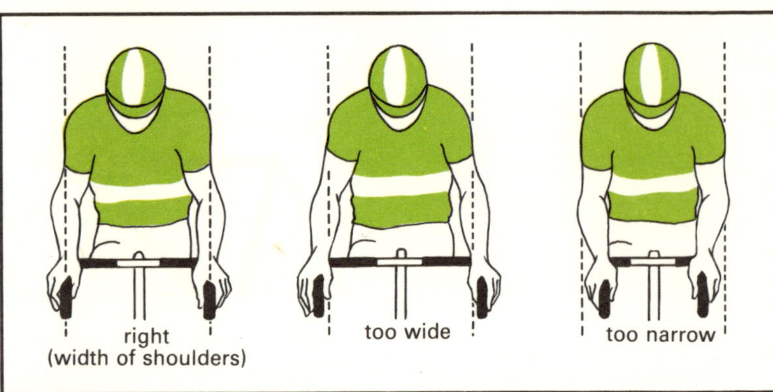

The following guidelines should be used for the length of the head set:

8-9cm with a frame height of 51-53cm
9-10cm with a frame height of 53-55cm
10-11cm with a frame height of 55-57cm
11-12cm with a frame height of 57-59cm
12-13cm with a frame height of 59-60cm

Racing handlebars – wide or narrow?

The different types of handlebars have already been discussed in the section on equipment. Their width is of interest here.

Handlebars are in fact made in different sizes.

The basic rule is that the handlebars must roughly correspond to the width of your rib cage.

In practice handlebar widths can be chosen according to the following points:

For narrowly built cyclists = 38cm
For normally built cyclists = 40cm
For big, powerful cyclists = 42cm

Handlebars that are too narrow hinder breathing and those that are too wide give an uncomfortable grip.

Raymond Poulidor, France's most popular cyclist – the 'eternal runner-up'. At the age of 40 he was still third in the Tour de France!

BP
MERCIER
HUTCHINSON
36
MERCIER

Cycling as a sport

Not only is there a choice of widths of handlebars; the offset length – the length of the curve and the vertical depth of the handlebars – can also be adjusted to suit any cyclist. But with spare-time cyclists this is rarely necessary.

The position of the foot on the pedal

The position of the foot on the pedal is extremely important for the transmission of power and leverage and therefore deserves special attention. Your foot is correctly placed on the pedal when the joint of the big toe, or the ball of the foot, is on the axis of the pedal. It's a really simple rule. So that the foot remains fixed in this position, there are cycle clips which, with the strap, produce a basket-like shape.

Here we must to some extent anticipate a cycling technique that will be discussed in detail later. The pedalling movement does not only consist of a pressing phase, but also a pulling phase. When the pedal is pulled upwards, your shoe – especially when going up steep inclines – moves out of the clip. Competitive cyclists therefore fit pedal grips or foot rests on the soles of their shoes. The shoe, pedal, cycle clip and pedal grip together form one unit. The length of the cycle clip and the siting of the pedal grip must be fixed in the correct relation to one another. This means that when the foot rest fixes the foot on the pedal, the end of the foot must push forwards into the cycle clip.

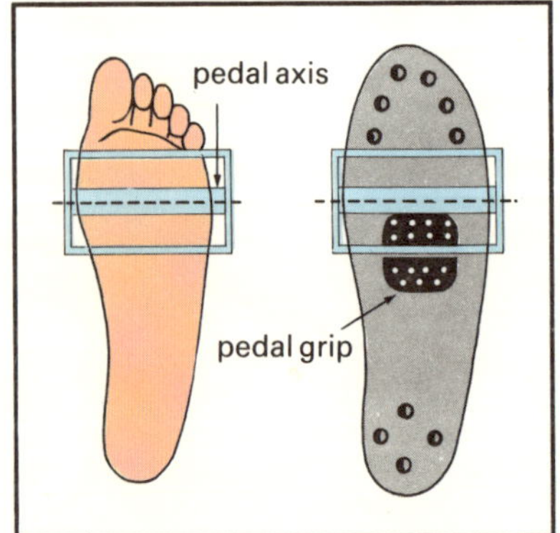

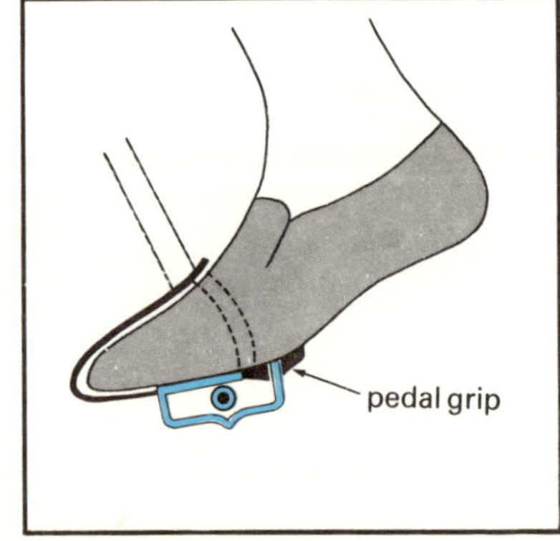

Racing cycle clips and pedal grips

shoe size	type of clip	depth of clip	shoe size	depth shoe is inserted
37	short	7.5 cm	37	10.0-10.5 cm
38	racing	7.5 cm	38	10.5-11.0 cm
39	clip	7.5 cm	39	11.0-11.5 cm
40	medium	8.5 cm	40	11.5-12.0 cm
41	racing	8.5 cm	41	12.0-12.5 cm
42	clip	8.5 cm	42	12.5-13.0 cm
43	large	9.5 cm	43	13.0-13.5 cm
44	racing	9.5 cm	44	13.5-14.0 cm
45	clip	9.5 cm	45	14.0-14.5 cm
46		9.5 cm	46	14.5-15.0 cm

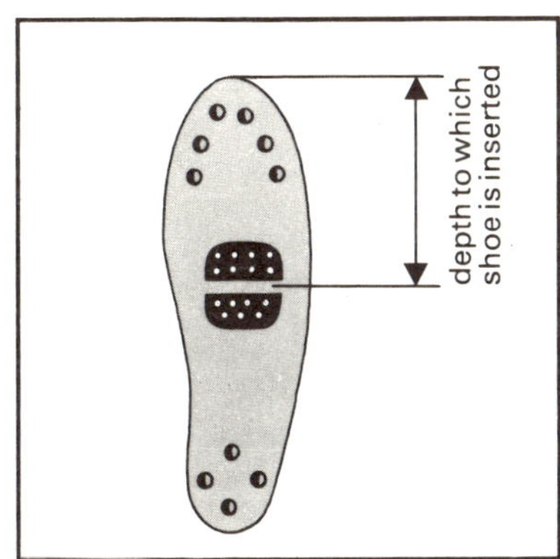

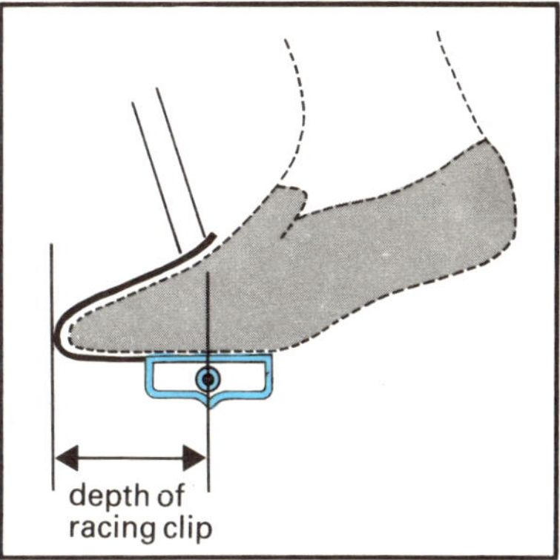

Cycling as a sport

Fitting the pedal grips, which should be done by the individual cyclist, requires the greatest precision. A pedal grip that is attached crooked lessens your pedalling ability and can lead to damage to your ankle or knee joints.

To find out the exact angle, first of all go cycling in new shoes a few times without fitting grips. The pedal leaves impressions on the sole of your shoe that will serve as an indication for positioning the grip on the sole. The foot seldom moves at right angles to the pedal. First fit the grips with only a few nails for a trial run. When you are quite sure of the exact position, you can fix them on to the sole of your shoes.

Procedure:

Coat the grip with adhesive and press on to the shoe, after leaving the adhesive a short while to dry.

Adjust the position as necessary.

Finally fix with available nails or small screws. If the soles are plastic, you will possibly have to drill holes first, using a thin bit. There are also types of shoe available where plastic or metal grips are already fitted to each shoe; these can be adjusted to suit the individual.

Transmission – gear rim and sprocket wheels

Transmission for the competitive cyclist is the relation between the perimeter of the sprocket wheels and the gear rim. This relationship determines the distance the cyclist covers in one revolution of the crank. The size of the sprockets and the gear rim is expressed according to the number of 'teeth'. A 20 gear rim therefore has 20 teeth. The greater the difference in teeth between the front sprocket and the gear rim on the rear wheel, the greater the transmission.

Therefore the distance the wheel covers in one crank revolution is also greater. The smaller the difference between the sprocket and gear rim, the smaller the transmission and therefore the distance covered in one crank revolution.

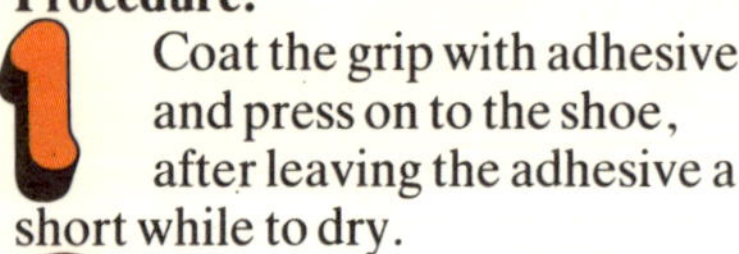

Rudi Altig was the most successful German professional cyclist on roads. In 1966 he became world champion on the Nürburgring.

Cycling as a sport

The perimeters of tyres and gear rims are given in inches. But for us conversion into metres is more relevant.

The following table shows the number of gear rim teeth horizontally and the tooth count of the sprocket vertically. You can get a reading in metres of the distance covered per crank revolution from the point where the relevant horizontal and vertical lines meet.

An example:

Sprocket 52
Gear rim 18 } = 6.17m

What is the correct transmission for you?

This depends on ability, form and the ground to be covered (hilly or flat). There are also very different aspects affecting this, so that you cannot set hard and fast rules. Only this one: beginners almost always use too great a transmission.

You can learn more on the subject of transmission in the section on **Cycling technique** on page 105.

The Italian Felice Gimondi became world champion in 1973. His victories include yet another in the Tour de France and three in the Giro d'Italia.

Transmission table for racing cyclists
(28 inches) (metres per crank revolution)

Number of teeth in gear rim

Number of teeth in sprocket:

	12	13	14	15	16	17	18	19	20	21	22	23	24	25	26
40	7.12	6.57	6.10	5.69	5.34	5.02	4.74	4.50	4.27	4.07	3.88	3.71	3.56	3.42	3.28
41	7.30	6.73	6.25	5.84	5.47	5.15	4.86	4.60	4.37	4.17	3.98	3.80	3.64	3.50	3.36
42	7.47	6.90	6.40	5.98	5.60	5.27	4.98	4.72	4.48	4.27	4.07	3.90	3.73	3.58	3.45
43	7.65	7.06	6.56	6.12	5.74	5.40	5.10	4.83	4.59	4.37	4.17	3.99	3.82	3.67	3.53
44	7.83	7.23	6.71	6.26	5.87	5.52	5.22	4.94	4.70	4.47	4.27	4.06	3.91	3.76	3.61
45	8.01	7.39	6.86	6.40	6.00	5.65	5.34	5.05	4.80	4.57	4.37	4.18	4.00	3.84	3.69
46	8.18	7.55	7.01	6.55	6.14	5.78	5.45	5.17	4.91	4.67	4.46	4.27	4.09	3.93	3.78
47	8.36	7.72	7.17	6.69	6.27	5.90	5.57	5.28	5.02	4.78	4.56	4.36	4.18	4.01	3.86
48	8.54	7.88	7.32	6.83	6.40	6.03	5.69	5.39	5.12	4.88	4.66	4.45	4.27	4.10	3.94
49	8.72	8.05	7.47	6.97	6.54	6.15	5.81	5.50	5.23	4.98	4.75	4.55	4.36	4.18	4.02
50	8.90	8.21	7.63	7.12	6.67	6.28	5.93	5.62	5.34	5.08	4.85	4.64	4.45	4.27	4.10
51	9.07	8.38	7.78	7.26	6.81	6.40	6.05	5.73	5.44	5.18	4.95	4.73	4.54	4.35	4.19
52	9.25	8.54	7.93	7.40	6.94	6.53	6.17	5.84	5.55	5.29	5.04	4.83	4.62	4.44	4.27
53	9.43	8.70	8.08	7.54	7.07	6.66	6.29	5.95	5.66	5.39	5.14	4.92	4.71	4.52	4.35
54	9.61	8.87	8.23	7.69	7.20	6.78	6.40	6.07	5.76	5.49	5.24	5.01	4.80	4.61	4.43
55	9.79	9.03	8.39	7.83	7.34	6.91	6.52	6.18	5.87	5.59	5.34	5.10	4.89	4.69	4.51
56	9.97	9.20	8.54	7.97	7.47	7.03	6.64	6.29	5.98	5.69	5.43	5.20	4.98	4.78	4.60

Cycling as a sport

Racing shoes

Competitive cyclists wear special shoes – and not just because of the pedal grips already fixed on. The uppers in this shoe are thin and soft, while the sole is relatively hard and stiff.

A hard sole has two advantages: firstly the teeth of the pedals do not dig into your feet. If you use gym shoes with soft soles over long distances, this can lead to marks on the balls of the feet. Secondly, a hard sole made of plastic or with a steel insert guarantees a better transmission of power.

It is extremely important for shoes to fit properly. If they are too big, the cyclist will lose some of the direct contact with the pedal.

For cooler weather, in spring or autumn, there are also higher, lined shoes to keep the feet warm, as well as low racing shoes.

Racing shorts

Black racing shorts are part of cycling – and not for reasons of fashion. Practice has shown that they are very important. Racing shorts cover at least one third of the thighs, thus stopping the saddle rubbing them raw.

A sewn-in leather insert is one characteristic of these close-fitting shorts. Cyclists wear the shorts next to the skin without underpants. The soft leather

Cycling shoes are available with smooth soles; the pedal grips are nailed on. There are also shoes with adjustable grips already fitted.

protects the thighs and seat from rubbing. You should wash them regularly to keep the material clean. Before training rub the inside of the leather with pure vaseline or cover it with powder. Many cyclists clean the leather once again with ether before greasing it. Extreme cleanliness avoids any inflammation. Therefore having a second pair of racing shorts is not a luxury. This enables you to change shorts when you train regularly, without having to worry about 'wet washing'.

Note: drying with too much heat stiffens the leather!

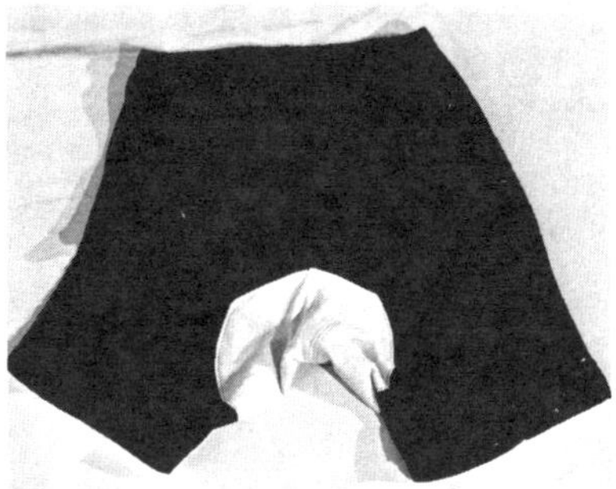

Always look after the suede of the seat so that it keeps its suppleness.

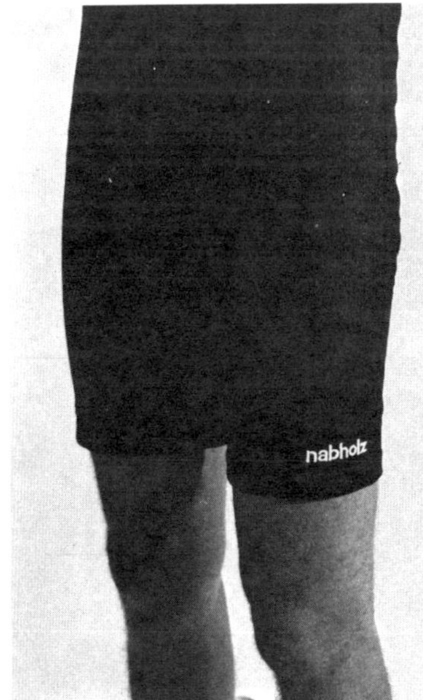

The shorts are kept up not only by the rubber waistband but also with braces (suspenders). A belt or a waistband that is too tight would only restrict breathing.

In cool weather you can wear ankle-length cycling trousers without leather inserts.

Black cycling trousers were certainly not chosen without a reason: even the weakest sun warms the legs at the coldest time of the year.

Cycling jersey

Adventurous, more or less tasteful colours provide cheerful splashes of colour in competitive cycling. Decorated with the names of manufacturers and the colours of the riders, they enable cycling fans to recognize from a distance their idols – Merckx,

Cycling as a sport

Gimondi, Hinault, Thurau or Braun. These jerseys are not just fashionable; they are also a warning on the roads – unfortunately almost totally dominated by motor traffic. Gaudy, easily visible coloured designs are important, particularly in the transitional period of early dusk. You are then that much easier seen by other road-users.

The material should be stretchy, should fit well without restricting movement and should absorb sweat. To protect the neck and shoulder muscles from cramp, a jersey collar that can close right up is indispensable. Cyclists wear jerseys with either short or long sleeves according to the weather.

One further feature of the cycling jersey is its length. The kidney area remains completely covered even when you bend down low. Pockets on the back, and possibly on the front too, are included on the racing jersey; provisions, money or maps can be stored in these. Many cyclists also put their spare tyre in one of these pockets.

Underclothes

You should wear a woollen or cotton vest under the jersey. For early evening or on cool days it is a good idea to wear a 'wind bib'. This thick linen bib, which is open at the sides, prevents the chest from cooling down during draughty descents after sweaty climbs. The wind bib has replaced newspaper, which cyclists used to pack under their jersey.

Jerseys must always be long enough to protect the back and kidneys.

Clothing

Racing cap

The traditional linen cap protects you against too much sun, absorbs sweat (which would otherwise run down into your eyes) and provides an easily visible mark for other road-users. There are special, thicker woollen caps for cold weather.

The wind bib protects against draughts and sudden cooling without causing a build-up of heat. You can wear the wind bib next to the skin, as shown here, but better still over a thin, absorbent vest (undershirt) made of wool or cotton.

Cycling as a sport

Gloves

In summer cyclists wear gloves with open fingers. The backs of the gloves are of open weave or knitted material and the palms are padded. This light padding softens any blows and prevents bruising. If you have a fall, the risk of injuring your hands is obviously reduced.

Experienced cyclists also use gloves during competitions to remove stones or other foreign bodies by wiping their hands over the tyres. But only those who really know how to do it should try this.

Crash hat

Cyclists are probably the most vulnerable road-users. They must protect themselves as much as possible – on the one hand by cycling defensively and in such a way as to prevent accidents, and on the other hand by taking their own protective measures. It is already compulsory for motorcyclists to wear protective headgear.

Especially when cycling in a group, cyclists are strongly recommended to wear a crash helmet made of plastic or a crash hat made of leather. In amateur cycle racing, the use of such protective headgear is

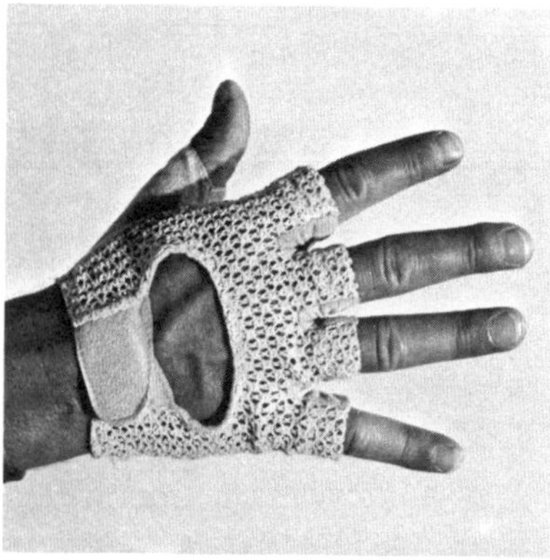

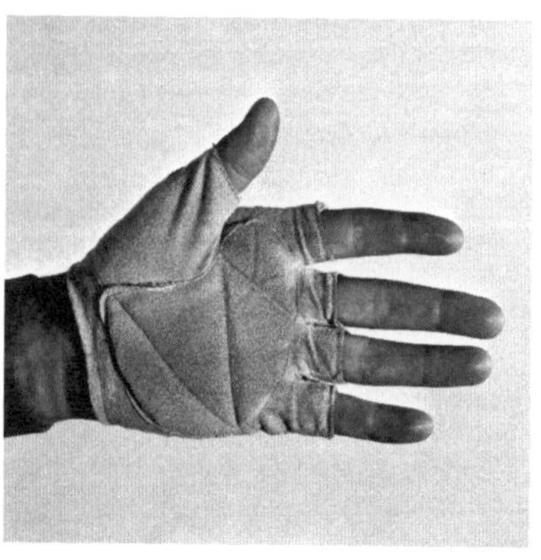

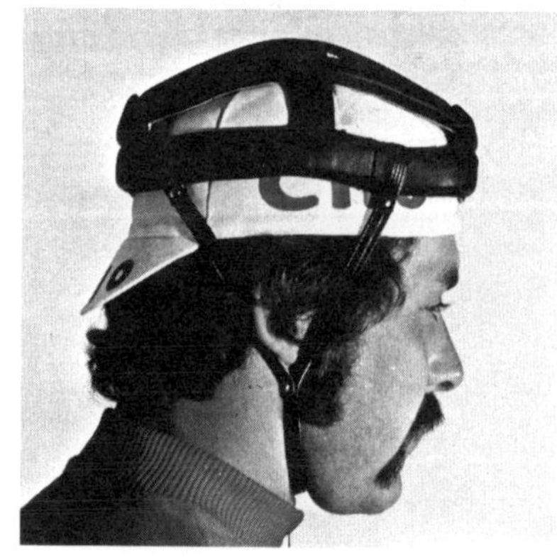

compulsory. Those who have experienced a crash will not laugh at this protective equipment.

Socks

Almost every type of sport has certain clothing rituals. In competitive cycling they are single-coloured (black) shorts and white socks. The upper part of the body is so brightly coloured that all competitive cyclists stick to this tradition.

The safety factor probably also plays a part in the colour of socks. Seen from behind, a cyclist's legs move up and down. Otherwise the body keeps relatively still. This movement is highlighted by gleaming white socks moving up and down, so that other road-users will see the cyclist more easily in poor light.

Correctly dressed for all weathers

Whereas in other types of sport mistakes in clothing do not have such a serious effect, in cycling problems are often very easily noticeable: colds, hardening of the muscles or inflammation of the nerves. Not everyone is as hardened as the road

Wearing a crash hat is compulsory for amateurs. Professionals also wear these valuable head protectors over difficult stretches.

professional. In the spring or autumn you can watch in astonishment as spare-time cyclists out in shorts and short-sleeved jerseys cycle past despite the cold. What may seem a pleasant temperature on a walk can turn out to be a cool breeze because of the airstream, which should not be underestimated. Experienced cyclists always suit their clothing to weather conditions.

Properly dressed

High summer

Racing cap (also wear sunglasses with unbreakable lenses).

Short-sleeved jersey with a vest (undershirt) underneath made of cotton or wool. For mountainous country, wear a wind bib between the underclothes and the jersey.

Rub sun tan lotion into your arms and legs.

Cycling shorts.

Spring/Autumn

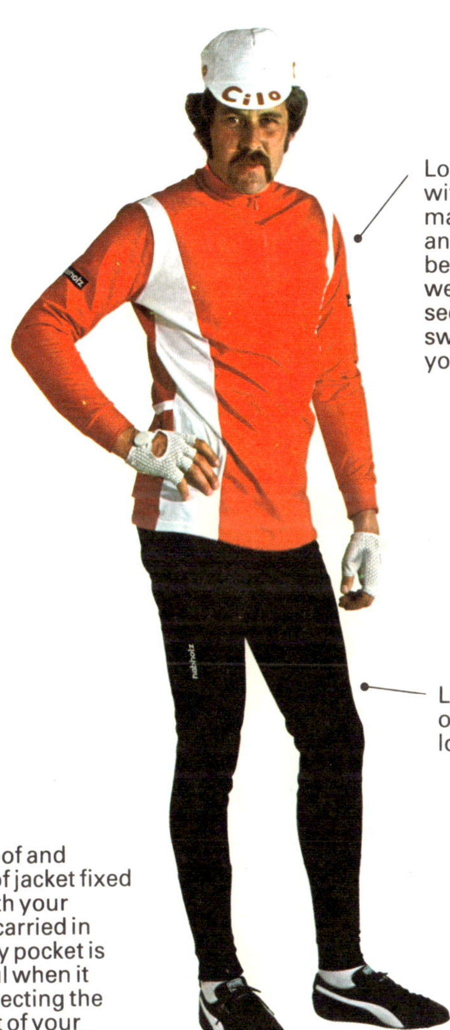

Long-sleeved jersey with a vest underneath made of cotton or wool and a wind bib in between. In colder weather wear a second, thin cotton sweater underneath your jersey.

Long cycling trousers or shorts with thin, long, over-trousers.

A windproof and waterproof jacket fixed underneath your saddle or carried in your jersey pocket is very useful when it rains, protecting the upper part of your body.

Properly dressed

Cold days

Woollen cap – thin linen caps do not keep you warm and if soaked through can affect the forehead.

Striking colours on your jersey are good for safety. The special cycling jacket keeps you warm and is particularly conspicuous on dull days. You can use a thick training jacket instead of a special jacket. (Cross-country skiers get good use from their skiing jackets, which protect them from the wind.)

Long cycling trousers are a must on cold days. If necessary, massage in an ointment that will stimulate the circulation in your legs.

If your feet get cold quickly, you can wear high-sided, lined shoes instead of the normal ones.

teka
eka
teka
7
teka

Looking after your racing bicycle

Just as car owners pay great attention to changing the oil, lubricating and waxing, cyclists should likewise look after their highly prized racing bicycles. This section cannot make cycle mechanics out of spare-time cyclists, but it can offer some guidance for those activities that you can easily carry out yourself. Basic tips on care have already been given in the section on **Cycling for pleasure**: cleaning the chain, cleaning the wheels and washing, oiling, replacing brake pads etc (see also page 15).

Left: Klaus Peter Thaler, cross-country world champion. Taking good care of your bicycle is obviously necessary in this especially tough variation of the sport.

What do you need as basic equipment?

- Set of open-ended spanners
- Set of ring spanners
- Combination pliers
- Petrol
- Repair kit
- Sponge, duster
- Tyre cement or adhesive tape
- Spoke key (nipple spanner)

Below:

1	Open-ended spanners
2	Ring spanners
3	Set of Allan keys
4	Tyre adhesive tape
5	Tyre cement
6	Combination pliers
7/8	Spoke keys
9	Tyre repair spray
10	Sponge
11	Screwdriver, toothbrush and old paint brush

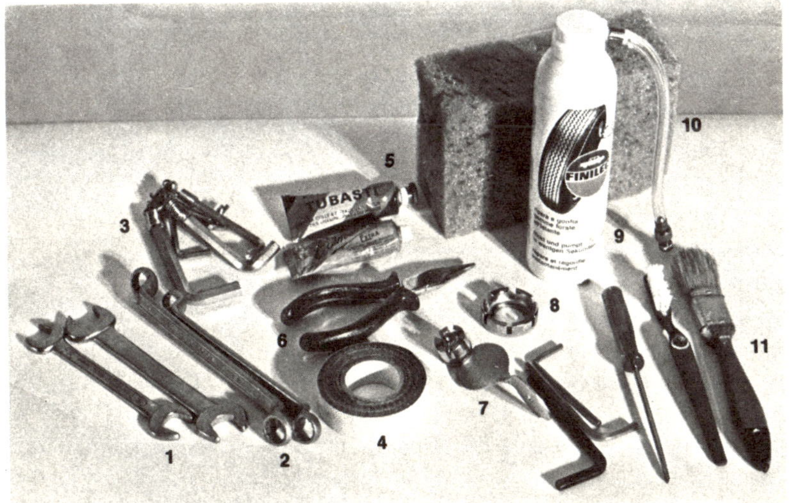

Cycling as a sport

Here we have limited ourselves to describing the most necessary work. Do-it-yourselfers will discover much more on their own racing bicycles and carry out repairs themselves which others would have to take to a mechanic. But it must be stressed to start with that those who tinker with their bicycle must proceed with extreme care and precision. Personal safety can depend on it. Carelessly tightened screws that come loose during cycling can lead to serious accidents.

Fitting a tubular tyre

Tyre kit or adhesive tape?

As already mentioned, the tubular tyre is stuck to the wheel rim. There are basically two possibilities:

- Gluing with adhesive tape to the wheel rim
- Gluing with a tyre kit

Preliminary work

New tyres are generally very stiff and difficult to fit over the wheel rim. You can make the job easier by stretching the tyre. For this, stand with your foot on the tyre and pull it up with your hands (do not rip it). Carry out this procedure all the way round, turning the tyre round after each pull. The expert fits it straight away on to the unprepared wheel rim to facilitate the 'real' fitting afterwards by stretching it more.

A new tyre can be well, but carefully, stretched before being pulled on; this makes fitting much easier.

Fitting a tyre

1/2 Pull off the old or damaged tyre – starting opposite the valve.

3   Put on adhesive tape.

4   Press the adhesive strip on firmly using a solid object.

2 To ensure good adhesion between the tape and the wheel rim, you must press it firmly on to the bed of the wheel rim. A round piece of wood or the handle of a screwdriver will do for this.

Gluing with adhesive tape on the wheel rim

1 The new wheel rim must be free of oil and grease. A quick wash with benzine or something similar will ensure this. Starting at the valve hole, fix the adhesive tape tightly on to the wheel rim – right round to the valve hole and overlapping it slightly. Make an opening for the valve, using a pointed object.

Cycling as a sport

3 There is a simple device for making it easier to take the tyre off later: stick a strip of paper or handlebar tape approximately 10cm long on to the adhesive tape opposite the valve. You can then pull off the tyre at this spot relatively easily without damaging the tyre.

4 Moisten as much as possible all the tape on the wheel rim. This prevents the tyre sticking too early. It also makes fitting it that much easier.

5 Now pull the slightly inflated tyre on to the wheel rim. Starting at the valve, which must be as straight as a die, pull the tyre down using both hands.

6 Without letting go, bring the wheel up to a horizontal position (on your thigh or on a table). Lift the remainder of the tyre over the wheel rim using pressure with your thumbs. Only tyres that have been stretched beforehand can be pulled on straight away with little trouble. Put on fresh adhesive tape after you have changed tyres two or three times.

Gluing with tyre cement

1 Gluing a tyre with cement requires care, cleanliness and practice. With a new wheel rim, degrease with benzine and then put on a layer of cement, allowing it to dry for 24 hours. Apply another two or three layers to give a good foundation of cement and ensure the tyre will stick on safely. Leave these extra layers for 10 hours to dry.

2 You need only leave the last layer (which should be put on the next day) for a short while, roughly 5-10 minutes, to dry. You can now pull on the tyre as for fitting with adhesive tape; but greater precision is needed. If you are not careful, you will get excess cement on the wheel rim, tyre and so on. Tyre cement can become brittle after some time; then you will have to put on some more.

Cycling as a sport

Alignment

1 Although the tyre is now firmly fitted on the rim, it is generally not quite round; alignment is therefore necessary. How do you trace the lopsided areas of the tyre? First pump it up slightly. Now hold the wheel on the right and left of its axis and give it a gentle push round. You will soon spot the lopsided areas where the tyre is not lying properly. The light-coloured sides can prove rather irritating as they almost never run parallel to the upper edge of the wheel rim. The shaped grooves provide a clue as to whether the tyre has been pulled on true or not.

2 Twist the lopsided areas of the tyre into the desired position using your thumbs and the ball of your fist. This requires a bit of practice. If you practise several times on an old tyre, alignment will soon become just a routine operation.

Note: you can use tyres which have been fitted with adhesive tape almost immediately (approximately after half an hour); cemented tyres should be left at least 8-10 hours to dry before use.

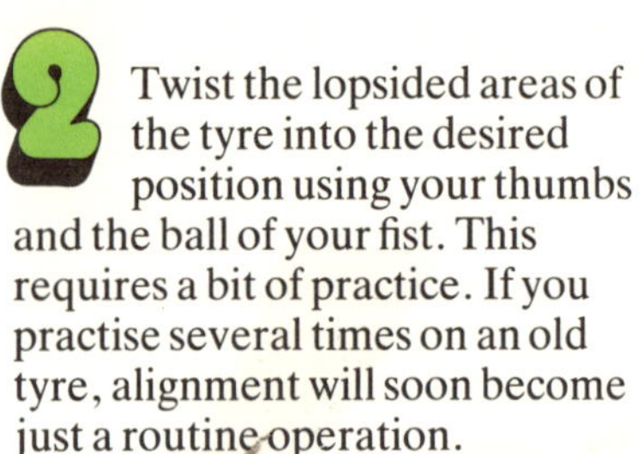

Amount of air

After aligning the tyres, pump them up to the normal pressure.

What is the normal pressure?
To achieve the optimum possible running, relatively high air pressure is required. Racing tyres lose pressure more quickly than normal training tyres. Check the air pressure before each trip. The normal pressure is between 50 and 60 lbs, but always check the recommended pressure depending on the tyre and the use to which it is being put. Check the amount of air using an air pump with a pressure gauge, a separate pressure gauge or with your hand. For this, place your thumb on the tyre and press down firmly using the ball of your fist. Since strength and feel are crucial here, this method can only be a rough guide: you should not under any circumstances be able to press the tyre in more than one quarter.

Cycling as a sport

How to align a wheel

With light racing wheel rims, lopsided holes or loose spokes can soon cause the wheel to lose its shape. You must check with an expert if the wheel is badly out of alignment; it may well be beyond repair. You need a lot of practice and the right touch to align a wheel precisely. But with a little skill you can carry out minor adjustments and align slight lopsidedness. We will not be discussing exact centering here. You will need a centering pillar or an old bicycle fork for this, which you mount on a wooden board. For easy adjustment, leave the tyre on the bicycle. If you give the wheel a light push, you will see where the adjustment is needed. You will have to put the bicycle on a stand to enable the wheel to turn freely.

Note the following basic principle:

The wheel rim will react as the spoke nipples are tightened or loosened.

Tighten the spokes opposite the 'list' to balance out the wheel rim. If the spokes are very tight, in some cases you will have to loosen them on the side of the 'list'. This must be done very carefully so as not to distort the wheel rim upwards; therefore

only give each spoke a quarter turn with the nipple spanner (spoke key). Also remember that to tighten you turn the spanner to the left (the opposite way screws are normally tightened), since the nipple is turned into the spoke – thus making it taut.

Therefore:
to tighten = turn to the left
to loosen = turn to the right

There are many types of spoke key. Proceed carefully with whichever model you are using, since alignment is a skill that has to be learnt with practice.

As you must certainly have realized by now, centering is quite a complicated task. Only the serious do-it-yourselfers should attempt it.

You should note one thing: with a new wheel or one that has had new spokes, some of the spokes will possibly work loose after a short time. You will probably have to make centering adjustments after you have covered 300-500km.

Tips and tricks

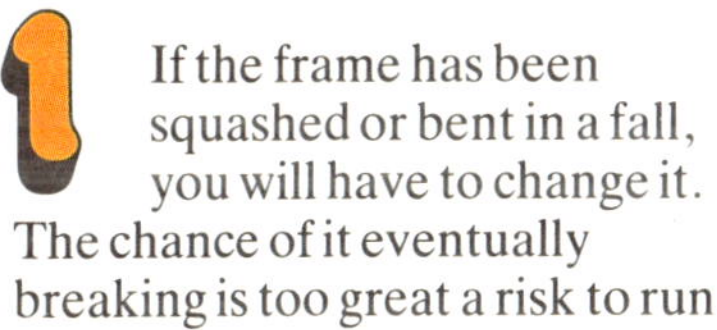

1 If the frame has been squashed or bent in a fall, you will have to change it. The chance of it eventually breaking is too great a risk to run.

2 To check whether your frame has been bent, cycle a short distance with no hands. If your frame is intact, the bicycle will run straight; a bent frame generally pulls the bicycle to one side. A further test is stretching a rope from the rear wheel fork to the head tube and back on the other side to the rear wheel fork. The saddle tube should be exactly between the two lengths of rope.

3 When straightening the handlebars after a fall, never put the front wheel between your legs and try forcing the handlebars into position. If the fastening screw on the head set has not been tightened too firmly, a blow with your hand on the end of the handlebars should be enough to straighten them again. If too much force is used, the inner clamp or the head set may be damaged.

4 There is a safety varnish you can use, which you paint on to screws to prevent nuts from loosening and falling off.

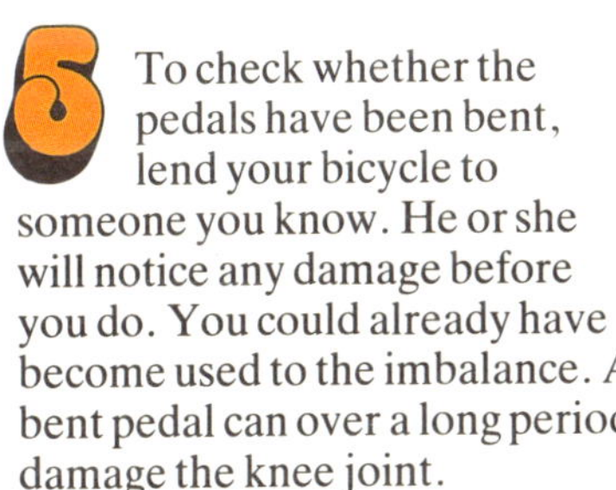

5 To check whether the pedals have been bent, lend your bicycle to someone you know. He or she will notice any damage before you do. You could already have become used to the imbalance. A bent pedal can over a long period damage the knee joint.

gas

Cycling technique

The sequence of movements in cycling is determined by the construction of the bicycle. However, competitive cyclists must observe a few criteria to be able to put their physical strength to maximum use.

A prerequisite for good technique is the correct sitting position. The details of this were described thoroughly in the section on **A bicycle to measure**.

Here are the most essential points again:

 **Correct saddle position, both in height and distance from handlebars**

 **Correct position of feet on pedals**

 **Correct length of pedal crank**

 **Correct handlebar adjustment**

Pay particular attention to the points of contact between your body and the bicycle – saddle, handlebars and pedals.

Gregor Braun on the track. This Olympic winner comes out on top because of his great strength and precise technique.

Pedalling

The rhythmical, neat footwork is called pedalling. This is how it works. The pedal on which your foot rests completes a 360 degree rotation around the axis of the pedal unit. The rotation is transmitted to the rear wheel through the chain. This produces forward movement. Cyclists make this sequence of movements automatically. The relationship between energy expended and performance depends on carrying out the pedalling process properly.

Closer examination will help us to understand the technique better. Unfortunately the sector in which the thigh moves downwards, achieving the greatest transmission of power, only amounts to two-fifths of the total rotation. If the pedal is at the lowest slack point after this phase, it must be brought up again. This happens automatically through the other pedal, which you simultaneously press downwards. However, this sequence of movements is 'angular'. Your foot must assume the important role and make a 'round' sequence of movements out of it. The pedalling movement, when examined in detail, is divided up into four sectors:

Cycling as a sport

The critical upper sector
In this phase, press forwards with the pedal in the horizontal position.

The sector of greatest power transmission
The thigh moves downwards, while the lower part of the leg and the feet stretch out. In this phase there is strong downward pressure.

The critical lower sector
The transition between the pushing and pulling phase comes about when the toes tilt downwards. This movement is extremely important and beginners must pay particular attention to it.

The sector of weakest power transmission
The sequence of movements in this phase separates beginners from experts more than any other. In fact your foot does not move passively upwards, but rather pulls. This greatly helps the pedalling downwards movement on the other side with the other leg.

This pulling movement is only possible if there is a firm link between the shoe and the pedal – by means of straps, racing clips and pedal grips.

This rhythmical and round sequence of movements is easy to achieve at low speeds. But if you are travelling very quickly, it becomes more difficult. Then the greatest demands are put on the agility of the joints. This rhythm should be practised to perfection. Only when the thrust-push-pull combination is right will you have achieved the most economical way of travelling, making optimum use of all the groups of muscles involved.

The diagram on page 103 clearly shows the groups of muscles involved in the pedalling process, through the different phases. If a group of muscles is over-strained due to unrhythmical, angular pedalling, the whole performance is adversely affected.

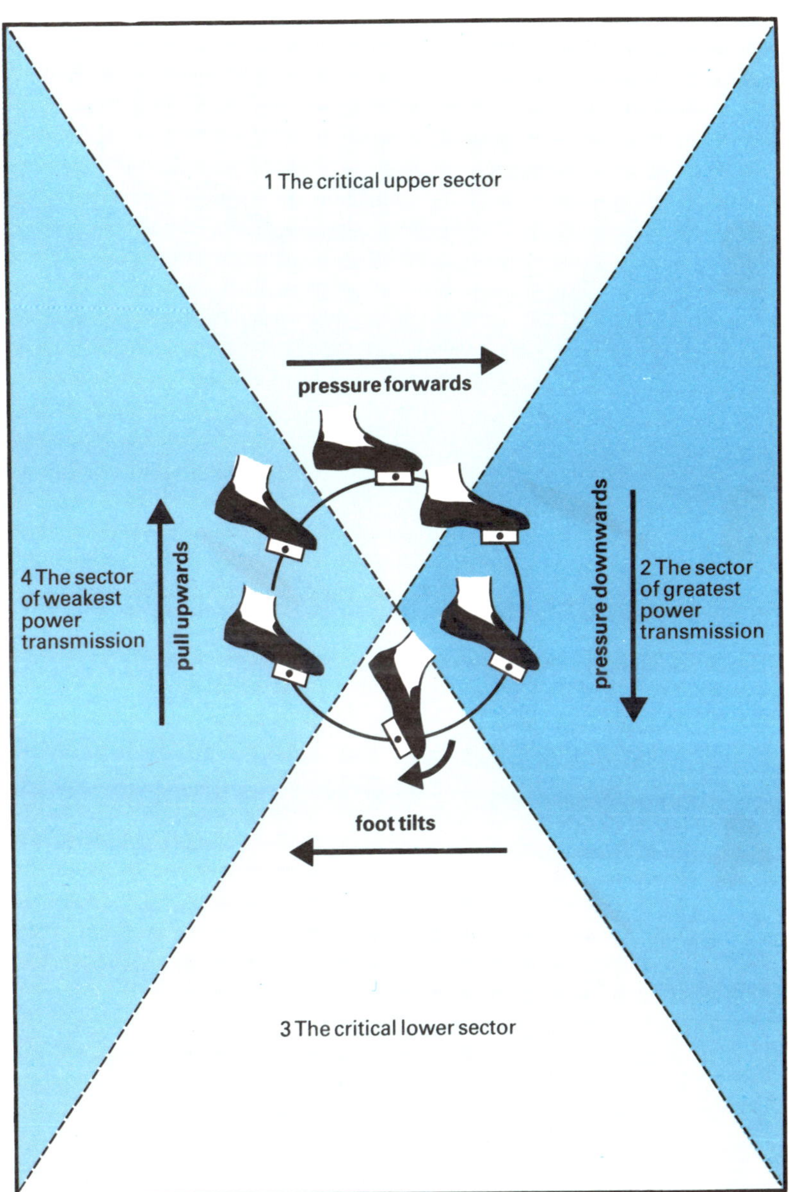

1 The critical upper sector
pressure forwards
pressure downwards
2 The sector of greatest power transmission
4 The sector of weakest power transmission
pull upwards
foot tilts
3 The critical lower sector

Cycling as a sport

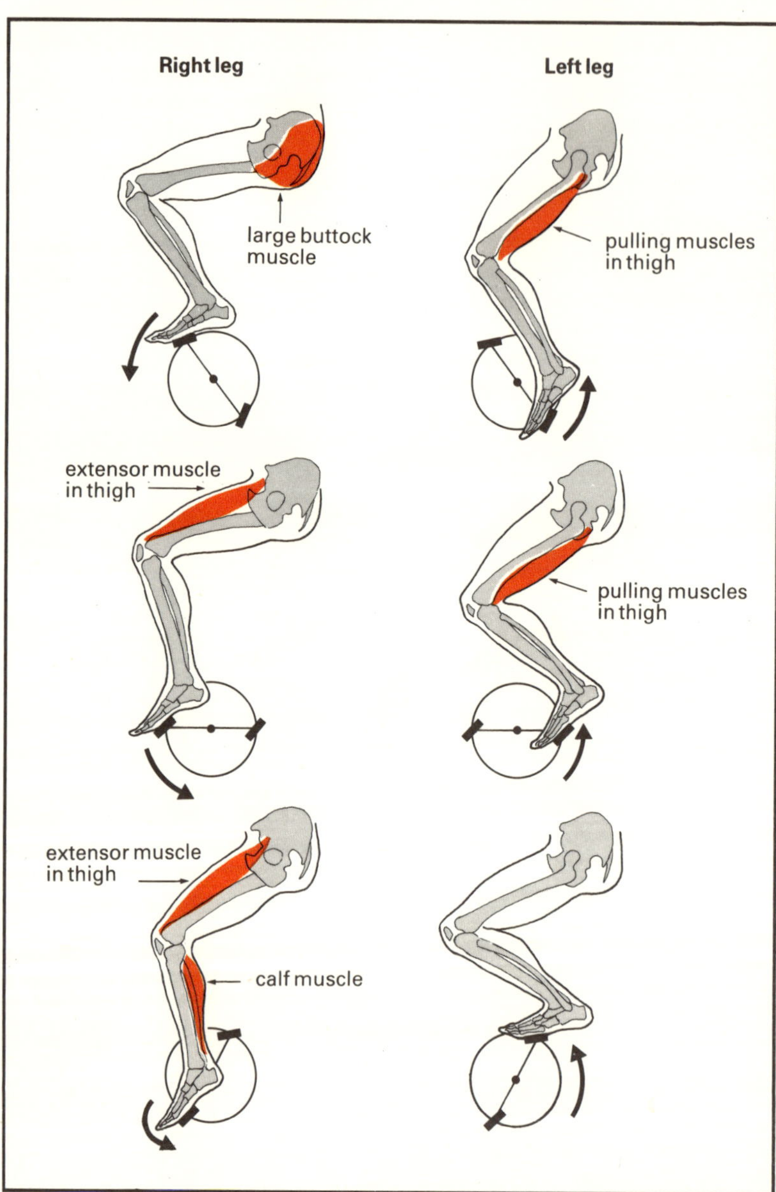

Using a rocking movement to pedal

You use the rocking movement on slopes when you cannot climb them sitting down, even using a lower gear. When starting off or sprinting, cyclists leave their saddles. You need to be quite athletic to use this method of pedalling. The strain involved in using the rocking movement through one revolution of the pedals can be compared to going upstairs two at a time.

The advantage lies in using the entire weight of the body on the front pedal, accompanied by pulling up the lower pedal; this means you can achieve greater acceleration. When carried out properly, the movement is supported by a 'pull' on the handlebars. These different requirements relieve some groups of muscles and make demands on others that are not used when cycling sitting down. Breathing is clearly improved compared to the lower sitting position.

Left: the diagram shows which groups of muscles are used in individual phases of the pedalling movement.

Below: Klaus-Peter Thaler using the rocking movement. A round trip like the Tour de France or the Giro d'Italia can only be won by someone who cycles well in hilly country.

Improving the pedalling movement

Some coaches make young cyclists ride up to 1000m using one leg only. Here is a slightly less strenuous way of training. The ground should be flat. Since there is no pressure from the second pedal, cyclists must concentrate much more on pulling upwards. Do this exercise first with the right leg and then with the left leg.

The choice of gear ratio

There is a reason for this to be discussed in the section on technique.

If you cycle with the wrong gear ratio, you cannot pedal properly. Your cycling rhythm should remain the same despite changes in the terrain. The gears are not there to boost the cyclist's strength but to keep the sequence of movements as regular as possible. Handling the gears properly should not be difficult if you are a car driver. You should not travel at too great a speed or too slowly in any gear; neither of these agrees with the car's engine – or, in the case of cycling, the cyclist's muscles.

The danger of choosing gear ratios that are too low rarely arises. On the contrary, most beginners in competitive cycling use gear ratios that are too high. If the gear ratio is too high, it will affect smooth pedalling and can lead to a hardening of the muscles. Frequent use of higher gears quickly leads to 'super-acidulation' of the muscles, with metabolic wastage and loss of agility.

Left: the Spaniard Frederico Bahamontes, the 'Eagle of Toledo', was the greatest climber, as mountain experts are called.

Below: the cyclist and his machine form a closed chain of levers. Upper part of the body: handlebars – hand – shoulder – hand – handlebars. Lower part of the body: pedal – leg – pelvis – leg – pedal.

Cycling as a sport

Changing gear correctly

The 10-gear mechanism is really an 8-gear mechanism

Avoid having the chain in extreme positions. These are: large sprocket in front and largest gear rim to the rear or small sprocket in front and the smallest gear rim to the rear. In these situations the chain will run too much at an angle and will cause the gear rim teeth to rub. This frictional resistance will naturally slow down your performance. Apart from this, there is more wear and tear on the parts (see the diagram below).

Correctly timed gear changing in hilly stages is crucial for professionals. If anyone makes a wrong change of gear, he or she quickly falls behind. Even those who cycle competitively as a hobby must learn to change gears at the right moment.

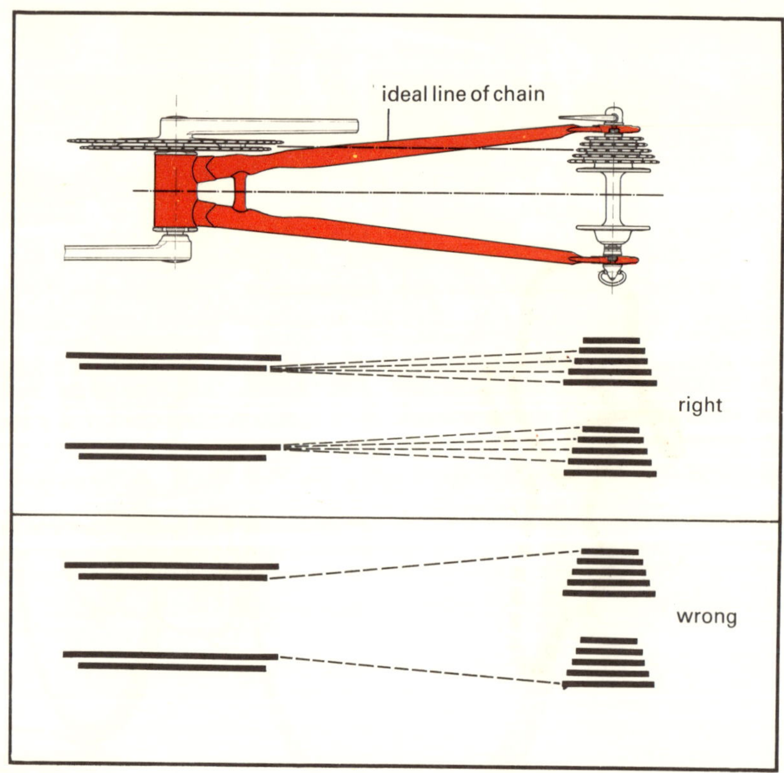

Cycling as a sport

The competitive cyclist frequently changes the position of the hands on the handlebars during a journey. There are three basic positions used according to the terrain and your speed.

At the bottom of the handlebars

You use the lower part of the handlebars in a head wind, for rapid sprints, when cycling in a slipstream, when going downhill or cycling in heavy traffic. In this way you are in the most favourable position aerodynamically, although breathing is made slightly more difficult. In heavy traffic, cycling downhill or cycling in a slipstream, this position is recommended since you can brake easily and stop quickly.

Hands over the brakes

Many cyclists cover the larger part of their journey in this position. Especially when cycling up hills, most experts prefer this way of holding the handlebars. According to the shape of the handlebars, cycling with your hands over the brakes is relatively comfortable and at the same time gives low wind resistance. The brake levers are then within relatively easy reach.

Hands on top of the handlebars

This position characterizes comfortable and relaxed cycling. Over-tensed muscles in the shoulders, neck and back can to some extent be relaxed in this position.

Cycling uphill

Change gear at the right time before the hill and tighten the straps on your racing clips. Grip from above, just over the brake levers. The correct breathing rhythm is even more important here than on flattish ground. People who do not breathe in and out sufficiently deeply soon become 'out of step' on hills.

Starting too quickly is not such a problem in normal countryside. But in hilly country it soon takes its toll. Your muscles become 'sour' and you can scarcely move the pedals. The skilled cyclist's secret lies chiefly in constantly changing from pedalling sitting down to pedalling out of the saddle. Those good at tackling hills cover many kilometres pedalling the cradle way, without sitting down.

Cycling up hills requires great muscular strength. People who attempt high hills when out of condition are acting extremely foolishly. Exercise of this type

Gripping the handlebars

Hands on top of the handlebars, giving a comfortable position for relaxed cycling.

Hands over the brakes, giving an aerodynamically favourable position that is still relatively comfortable.

Hands below on the handlebars to afford less wind resistance (for sprints, against head wind and when cycling in a slipstream).

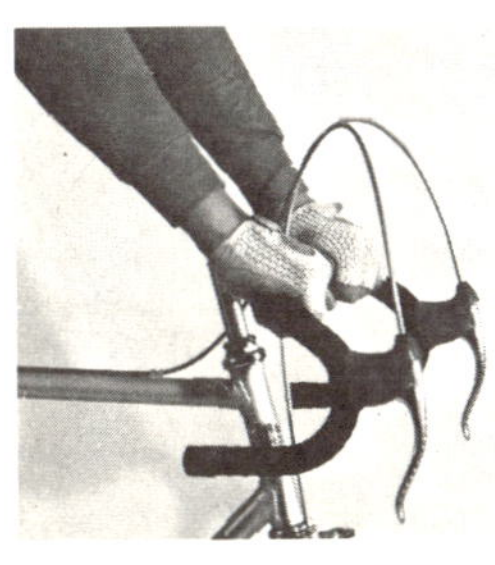

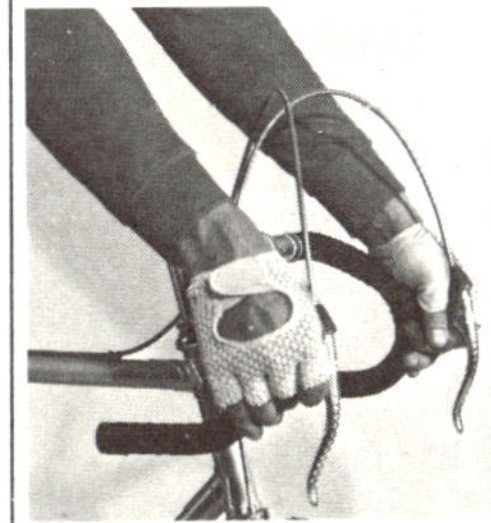

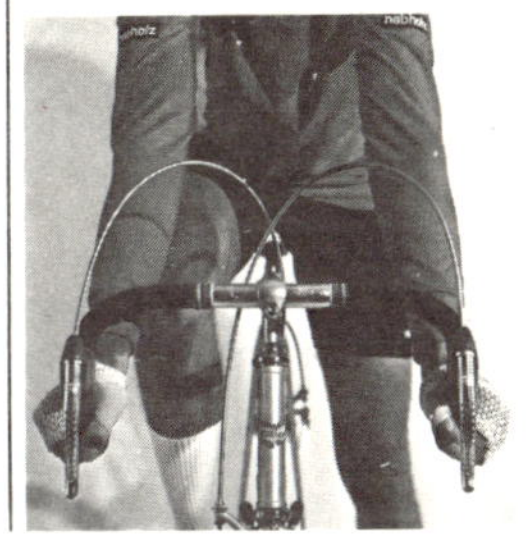

can very quickly lead to overstrain. You cannot reach top condition overnight. It is absolutely vital to increase your exercises slowly and continuously.

Brake – but gently

In cycling some falls are due entirely to faulty braking technique. Always apply the front and back brakes at the same time. Then slowly increase the pressure on the brakes. This way you will achieve effective braking progressively, without skidding. Reduce speed before bends by braking gently. If you brake on a bend, the tyre can lose its equilibrium through lack of adhesion.

Everything becomes much more difficult on wet roads. The brake rubbers lose a large amount of effect on wet wheel rims. To slow down confidently and safely, you should allow double the normal braking distance. Since the danger of skidding is substantially increased on wet roads, sudden braking is very dangerous. The basic principle of gentle braking at the right time applies even more here.

The technique of cycling in a slipstream has to be learnt. Cyling in close formation as demonstrated here by professionals is too dangerous for those who only cycle as a hobby.

Cycling as a sport

Cycling round bends

Do not cycle too rigidly when taking bends. 'Keep close in to all bends so as not to be carried out' is the maxim. But cutting corners as practised by professional cyclists is very dangerous. For those whose profession is cycling, it is one of the risks they run and in major races the roads have barriers for motor traffic.

Here is another tip on pedal position. On straight stretches of road the pedals must be in a horizontal position. On bends the inner pedal should always be on top: left-hand bend – left pedal on top; right-hand bend – right pedal on top. If the reverse happens, the pedal will touch the ground and you will fall off.

Cycling in a slipstream

With one or more training partners you can take turns to lead. Air resistance is substantially reduced if you travel in a slipstream and pedalling becomes easier. For those who cycle competitively as a hobby, only one method of travelling in a slipstream is really applicable: cycling closely one behind the other. Echelon formations in which cyclists are staggered, for example to the side because of a side wind, are not possible in heavy traffic. Formations of this type are only possible and safe in racing. A distance of a few centimetres from the person in front naturally gives the best results, but requires good cycling technique and very quick reactions. There is less danger if you keep to a safe distance apart.

You should follow certain rules when cycling one behind the other:

 Watch traffic carefully before relieving the leader.

 The leader should make it known that he or she wants to change by means of a signal. This reduces the danger of a collision.

Cycling technique

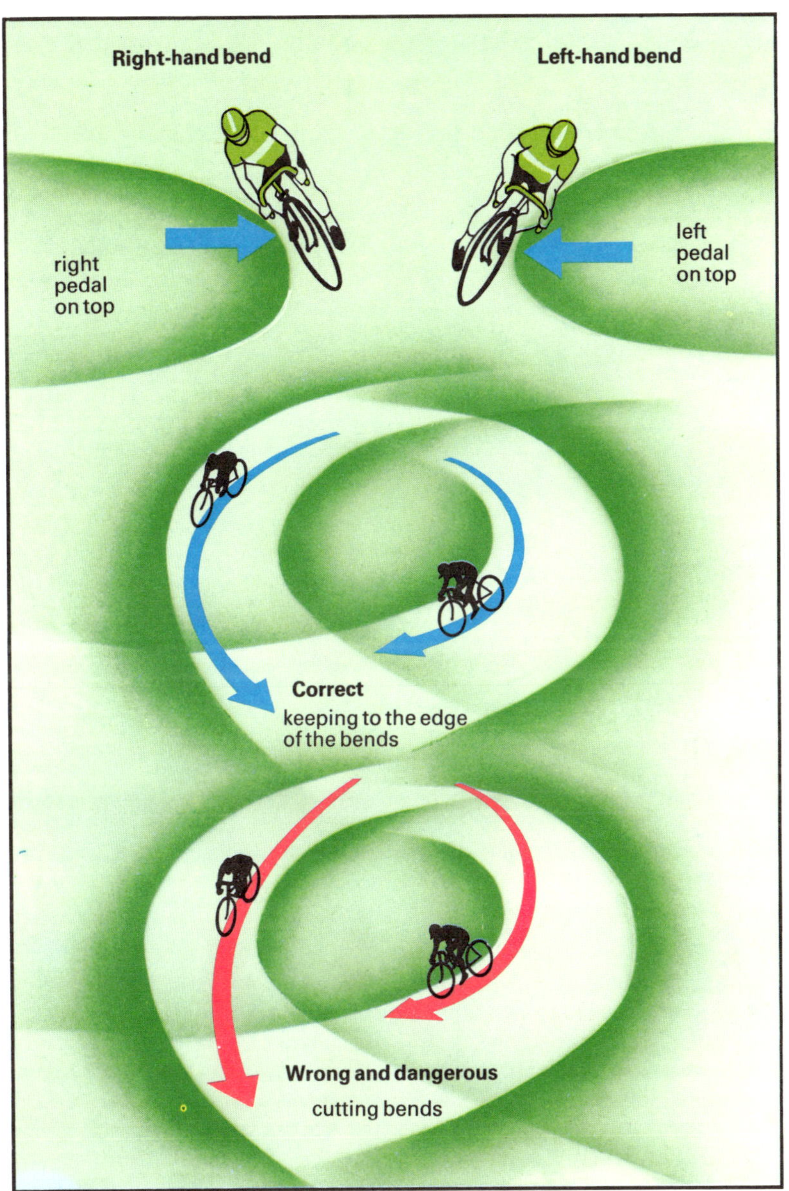

Cycling as a sport

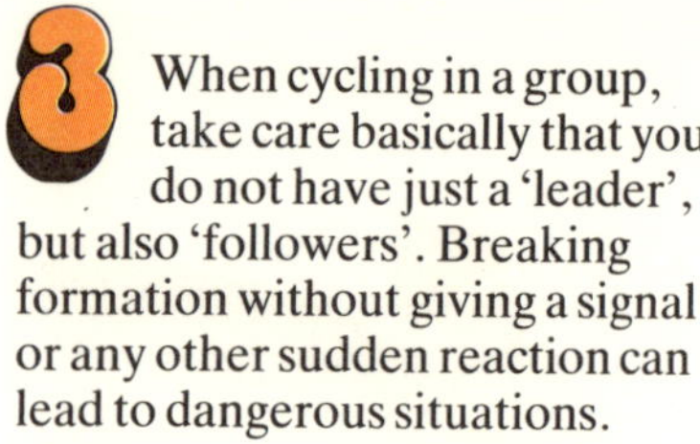

When cycling in a group, take care basically that you do not have just a 'leader', but also 'followers'. Breaking formation without giving a signal or any other sudden reaction can lead to dangerous situations.

The stronger the head or side wind, the more frequently you should change positions.

When cycling in a slipstream, use the low cycling position. Put your hands on the lower part of the handlebars, with your fingers on the brakes ready to react.

The person who takes over the leadership must watch out that the others stay close. An excessively fast start could break up the group.

Checking your bicycle before the start

A racing bicycle is a piece of complicated machinery which needs to be checked over. In particular, the brake screws must be checked so that no dangerous situations can arise. A racing cyclist naturally uses the machine more heavily; therefore it should be looked after all the the more carefully. Success will, to an extent, depend on its condition.

The spare tyre

As already mentioned in the section on equipment, you should always carry a spare tyre. To avoid any unwelcome surprises, you should take it out of its bag or leather case regularly and pump it up. Otherwise the rubber will become fragile at the creases and will not be airtight.

Looking after your physical well-being

This section is of special significance if you want to avoid injury. Here are the most important principles:

The right clothing for the weather conditions is imperative if you are to avoid muscle damage and colds.

Look after your trousers after cycling in the rain. Dirt that is ingrained into the wool can lead to inflammation. Treat the inside of the leather with vaseline cream or rub powder on to it. Sensitive cyclists put vaseline on the whole backside area before training.

Before and after the training run

3 If, in spite of these precautions, you are still sore, taking cold hip baths, cleaning with washing soap and applying good skin ointments will help. In extreme cases, give up training for a short while and switch to another type of sport.

4 After training take a shower, with the water at body temperature. In this situation cold water is painful to the muscles; but a short, cold shower afterwards will not hurt.

5 Wash eyes inflamed by sweat and dust with an 'eye bath' (which you can get from chemists). Sensitive cyclists should take the precaution of wearing spectacles. You can absorb sweat running from your forehead by wearing a cap.

6 There can be many reasons for muscle cramp: over-straining muscles through insufficient training, the use of too great a transmission ratio, a bad sitting position or a high salt loss on hot days and during prolonged exercise. In the case of mild cramp, switching to a lower transmission ratio and changing your sitting position by moving back in the saddle will often help.

If the cramp is more severe, try to alleviate it by gentle massaging and taking salt tablets to restore the mineral balance (in hot weather).

Cold weather and insufficient clothing can also lead to cramp. In a case like this, rubbing in something to encourage the circulation will lessen the danger of cramp.

Food

Cycling numbers among the types of sport with the highest consumption of calories.

The daily requirements of cyclists in a stage race amounts to 6000 calories. Cyclists who only compete in their spare time rejoice over this paunch-reducing factor. Energy consumption quickly increases at high speeds. Calorie consumption at a speed of 21km/hr and 70kg body weight amounts to 610 calories, and at 30km/hr 840 calories.

Cycling as a sport

Before training

Your last meal time should be about an hour and a half before training starts. If that is not possible because, for example, cycling begins early in the morning, experienced cyclists at least have light, filling fare such as muesli or a similar food. Taste and the ability to digest vary a lot here, so proper nourishment must be suited to the individual.

Refreshments during training

'Eat before you are hungry and drink before you get thirsty'
This says everything there is to say about nourishment when training. On short runs you can easily manage without food or drink. But when training over a distance greater than 60km, a 'calorie reinforcement' is necessary during that period. Lots of small helpings are much better than one big one. Every 30-40 minutes cyclists should eat a small amount. If you eat small amounts regularly, you will not become prey so easily to weakness caused by lack of nourishment or to hunger pains. Also, a rapid lowering of the blood sugar level can, in extreme cases, lead to dizziness or fainting.

The following are suitable for spare-time competitive cyclists as food during training: dried fruit, peeled oranges, bananas, rice pudding, fruit cake, chocolate, bread with cheese or ham.

Basically everything is packed in small portions (preferably in aluminium foil) to facilitate eating while cycling.

For liquid refreshment there are a host of 'secret mixtures'. Here are two examples:

1 For hot days
Juice of 3 lemons, 150g glucose, 2 egg yolks and 2g cooking salt; whisk together and top up the drinking bottle with water.

2 For cool days
350g gruel, 120g glucose, 4 egg yolks and 2g cooking salt.

Eddy Merckx picking up his 'flying' refreshments. Numerous falls have resulted from confusion between cyclists and attendants.

Cycling as a sport

After topping up the balance of calories, replacing fluid is at least as important. In hot weather racing cyclists can lose 2 or 3 lbs in sweat in an hour. Loss of sweat also entails loss of minerals. Today doctors recommend drinking sufficient amounts at the right time. Not drinking, which used to be practised in various endurance sports, has been proved to be wrong.

If you are liable to get cramp, it is as well to carry salt tablets as well as normal refreshments.

These preparations, which are well-known in other sports, are easily taken and, if used at the right time, can prevent muscle cramp or clear it if it is already present.

After training

The fluid loss that cannot be made up sufficiently during exercise must be compensated for as quickly as possible afterwards. Heavy, greasy meals are not recommended after strenuous training since they restrict digestion. Many sportsmen and women do not have any appetite for lavish meals immediately after training. They would much rather have light meals that are rich in carbohydrates.

Special training for competitive cyclists

Here are a few training tips for anyone who wants to improve his or her ability. Basically, you have to keep yourself fit the whole year. There is a section on this called **Compensatory sport/ winter training** (see page 120). Most cyclists give cycling a winter break. You should, however, put special value on organizing training in the spring and getting accustomed to the bicycle again.

Training Stage 1 (4 weeks)

Round pedalling

In this stage cyclists should train as far as possible 2-3 times per week using low gear ratios. Avoid steep inclines. Keep sitting on gentle slopes and try to improve your style – not strength. Cycle uphill without using your arms – therefore without any pulling movements on the handlebars. Your hands should lie loosely on the handlebars.

Training Stage 2
(4 weeks)

Rhythm and muscle-building
Slowly increase the gear ratio.
But gentle pedalling should still
remain your main goal. For
strength training, cover uphill
sections of 100m, 200m, 300m
and 400m standing up.

Stamina and speed, in
particular, should be developed
in the last two weeks of this stage
of training.

Stamina runs twice a week
This is not just a question of
covering a lot of kilometres; you
must also accustom yourself to
exercises of long duration. Cycle
with medium gear ratios, still
keeping a watch on your style,
rhythm and breathing. In stamina
training your pulse rate should
not be more than 130.

Speed training once a week
These training runs should be
short and completed using higher
gear ratios, after warming up. So
as not to 'sour' your muscles
quickly, 3-4 runs – ending every
300m – are recommended for

Cycling as a sport

speed training. Pedalling should not lose its rhythm or become cramped in spite of the high speed.

Training Stage 3 (3 weeks)

Rhythm and muscle-building
In this period you should have two long and two short runs in the weekly training schedule.

Longer run: warm up for 10-15 minutes. Cycle several times at very high speeds over a period of 2-10 minutes. Reduce recovery periods in between from 5 to 2 minutes. Finish with a gentle run of 10-15 minutes.

Increase the duration of the rapid periods continuously in progressive training.

Sprint training:
After 10-15 minutes warming up, practise sprints over 300-500m distances. Include at least 4-5 sprints per session.

Training Stage 4

If you have no racing ambitions, keep training roughly to the first three stages. If you get overtired after a training run, the next training session should not have the same effect. A cyclist in training will quickly recover during an easy cycling trip.

Medical supervision

Cyclists who compete in races have to undergo regular medical examinations. Spare-time cyclists over 35 or those who haven't had any exercise for several years should definitely seek medical advice before beginning their training and be re-examined every year.

Compensatory sport and winter training

There are weather conditions that make it no fun to do cycle training (when it rains, for example) or can lead to too much exposure (at temperatures below 0°C). In regions of constantly changing weather, the competitive cyclist should certainly look for an alternative sport to make up for any enforced breaks.

Training for the whole year

Racing cyclists cannot manage with long breaks from training. Even in bad weather they train or exercise on special 'rolling road' machines, either at home or at their club headquarters. There are various systems. The most frequently used piece of apparatus is one in which the rear wheel runs on two rollers and the front wheel on one; in this case a normal bicycle can be used. This special equipment is only of interest to racing cyclists.

There are other possibilities for spare-time cyclists. Sports that make demands on your stamina are the most valuable: running throughout the year and cross-country skiing in winter, for example.

Running

Running for exercise is possible the whole year in any weather and improves your physical ability. This type of exercise quickly shows good results. Hardened muscles can very quickly be loosened up with light running.

Training

A so-called 'running game' in open country as hilly as possible comes closest to cycling exercises. After warming up, intersperse short and long increases in tempo with slow trotting or walking breaks. You should conclude a running game like this with at least 15 minutes of relaxed trotting.

Various parts of the countryside should be used as far as possible (rises, slopes, bending in between trees etc). Jogging can be done over longer distances at as even a tempo as possible. Do not exceed a pulse rate of 150.

Training in winter

Cross-country skiing

Like cycling, this winter sport takes place over long distances. Moreover, your whole body from your fingertips to your toes is thoroughly exercised. When cycling in hilly country, cyclists benefit especially from exercising their arm muscles. Even the cycling greats – Eddy Merckx, Felice Gimondi etc – keep up their form by cross-country skiing and it is firmly part of the winter training régime for many national or professional teams. Cross-country training, if carried out competitively over hilly country, can correspond to cycling exercises. The runner's body is subjected to constantly changing exercise due to inclines and descents. The leg muscles are exercised in a slightly different way, but the heart and blood circulation are put to very good use. Competitive cyclists will feel the enormous effect of cross-country skiing, especially on runs in hilly country, in the following summer.

Training

You can train happily for several hours without any great strain on your system. You will avoid excess strain on bones, ligaments and tendons because of the gliding movement.

Any forms of training are possible. Using the countryside, you can incorporate exercises in which the pulse rate changes. As well as flat stretches, most cross-country regions have various inclines and descents. This is ideal training for long cycle runs the next summer.

We cannot go into detail in this book about the equipment, technique and training for cross-country skiing. Special literature is required for this. It is worth getting to grips with this subject, since cross-country skiing looks fun, but actually requires intensive training if you are to achieve the best technique.

Cross-country skiing – an excellent substitute sport during the winter.